LIGUORI CHRISTIAN INITIATIC

FOR ADULTS

CATECHUMENATE LEADER GUIDE

Journey of Faith for Adults Catechumenate Leader Guide (827167)

Imprimi Potest: Stephen T. Rehrauer, CSsR, Provincial, Denver Province, the Redemptorists

Imprimatur: "In accordance with CIC 827, permission to publish has been granted on ?, 2016, by the Rev. Msgr. Mark S. Rivituso, Vicar General, Archdiocese of St. Louis. Permission to publish is an indication that nothing contrary to Church teaching is contained in this work. It does not imply any endorsement of the opinions expressed in the publication; nor is any liability assumed by this permission."

Journey of Faith © 1993, 2005, 2016 Liguori Publications, Liguori, MO 63057.

To order, visit Liguori.org or call 800-325-9521.

Liguori Publications, a nonprofit corporation, is an apostolate of the Redemptorists. To learn more about the Redemptorists, visit Redemptorists.com. All rights reserved. No part of this publication may be reproduced, distributed, stored, transmitted, or posted in any form by any means without prior written permission.

Contributing writers and editors of 2016 *Journey of Faith for Adults Catechumenate Leader Guide*: Denise Bossert and Julia DiSalvo. Design: Lorena Mitre Jimenez. Images: Shutterstock.

Unless noted, Scripture texts in this work are taken from *New American Bible*, revised edition © 2010, 1991, 1986, 1970 Confraternity of Christian Doctrine, Washington, D.C., and are used by permission of the copyright owner. All Rights Reserved. No part of the *New American Bible* may be reproduced in any form without permission in writing from the copyright owner. Excerpts from English translation of the *Catechism of the Catholic Church for the United States of America* © 1994 United States Catholic Conference, Inc. —*Libreria Editrice Vaticana*; English translation of the *Catechism of the Catholic Church: Modifications from the Editio Typica* © 1997 United States Catholic Conference, Inc. —*Libreria Editrice Vaticana*. Compliant with *The Roman Missal, Third Edition. Modern Catholic Dictionary* by Fr. John A. Hardon, SJ © 1999 Eternal Life.

Printed in the United States of America.
20 19 18 17 16 / 5 4 3 2 1
Third Edition

Contents

The Catechumenate: A Period and Process

Rites Belonging to the Catechumenate 4

Sponsors and Godparents:
Knowing and Making the Difference 6

Effective Catechesis during the Catechumenate........6

Practical Suggestions 7

Integrating the Parish Community 7

Catechumenate Lesson Plans

C1. The RCIA Process and Rites

C2. The Sacraments: An Introduction

C3. The Sacrament of Baptism

C4. The Sacrament of Confirmation

C5. The Sacrament of the Eucharist

C6. The Sacrament of Penance and Reconciliation

C7. The Sacrament of Anointing of the Sick

C8. The Sacrament of Matrimony

C9. The Sacrament of Holy Orders

C10. The People of God

C11. The Early Church

C12. Church History

C13. Christian Moral Living

C14. The Dignity of Life

C15. A Consistent Ethic of Life

C16. Social Justice

Catechumenate Glossary 104

The Catechumenate: A Period and a Process

Since the time of the early Church, generally "the catechumenate" referred to the entire process of Christian conversion and initiation. It spanned multiple years and involved formal instruction, acts of penitence, and public rites that confirmed the community's approval as well as the catechumen's changed status.

Today, the term *catechumenate*, and *catechumen* in some respects, refers to a specific stage within the typical RCIA process. The rite of acceptance has been called a "first step" even though most participants take part in a period of inquiry as well as unknown years of personal discernment before contacting a Catholic parish (*RCIA* 42). And while the rite of election technically "closes the period of the catechumenate proper," catechumens (then the *elect*) and candidates continue to meet for months and have not yet been fully initiated (*RCIA* 118; see also *National Statutes for the Catechumenate*, 6).

The period of the catechumenate remains at the heart of the RCIA process. Team members, catechists, and participants should take advantage of all its benefits and allow it to progress naturally. Especially when an inquirer enters the process later than others, Lent arrives early, or there are exceptional circumstances, it may be best to extend the length of this period rather than rushing through or shortchanging the participant's needs and experiences.

While the catechumenate is distinctly reserved for more formal instruction and presentation of essential doctrine, it is also a time for participants to practice and apply their faith. The Church identifies four goals for the catechumenate (*RCIA* 75). During this period, participants will:

1. receive a "suitable catechesis…planned to be gradual and complete in its coverage.…This catechesis leads the catechumens not only to an appropriate acquaintance with dogmas and precepts but also to a profound sense of the mystery of salvation…" (see also Decree on the Church's Missionary Activity Church [*Ad Gentes*], 14, from the Second Vatican Council).

2. "become familiar with the Christian way of life…, learn to turn more readily to God in prayer,… and to practice love of neighbor, even at the cost of self-renunciation."

3. participate in "suitable liturgical rites, which purify the catechumens little by little and strengthen them with God's blessing.…At Mass they may also take part with the faithful in the Liturgy of the Word, thus better preparing themselves for their eventual participation in the liturgy of the Eucharist."

4. "learn how to work actively with others to spread the Gospel and build up the Church.…"

Throughout the catechumenate, catechumens and candidates will undergo "a progressive change of outlook and morals" (*AG* 13). RCIA leaders and sponsors can be catalysts for this spiritual transformation by providing opportunities for reflection, interaction with the community, and by supporting their study with clear and accurate information. Many features of the *Journey of Faith* program and materials assist you in achieving those goals.

Prior to the rite of election, leaders, sponsors, and participants themselves should observe an increase in the participant's understanding and ownership of his or her Catholic Christian faith. The signing of names into the *Book of the Elect* signifies the fuller "yes" to Christ and Church that began in his or her heart at the rite of acceptance.

Rites Belonging to the Catechumenate

Celebrations of the Word of God

The catechumenate, indeed the entire RCIA process, is connected intrinsically to the liturgical year. The Church's recommendation that the RCIA process last at least one year is to ensure that catechumens experience the fullness of the paschal mystery as reflected in the liturgy.

Many RCIA groups attend the Sunday Liturgy of the Word together. Others meet during the week to proclaim and reflect on the upcoming readings. You may combine these celebrations with the catechetical sessions or keep them separate. However you structure your RCIA process, maintaining a connection to the seasons of the Church year and regularly, prayerfully breaking open the Scriptures is vitally important. *The Word Into Life*—available in three volumes for Sunday Cycles A, B, and C—provides the full text of the readings along with commentaries and questions for an RCIA audience.

Model for a Celebration of the Word of God

1. *Song.* The celebration opens with an appropriate hymn or chant.

2. *Readings and Responsorial Psalm.* A baptized member, ideally a trained lector, proclaims a reading or two from Scripture. As in Mass, the first or Old Testament readings are followed by a psalm, either sung or in call-and-response format.

3. *Homily.* The RCIA director, pastor, or another trained homilist or catechist briefly explains and applies the readings.

4. *Concluding Rites.* The celebration closes with a prayer or one or more of the optional rites below (*RCIA* 85–89).

Optional Rites

Catechumens and candidates can be nourished by other liturgical rites during this period. The Church offers texts and guidelines for minor exorcisms (petitions for strength in the challenges of faith and struggle against temptation), blessings, and anointings, which may occur on their own or conclude a celebration of the word (*RCIA* 90–103). Speak to your priest or deacon about when and how these might benefit your particular group.

Also, you will need to determine what rites are appropriate for the period of enlightenment and how they will fit into the weeks leading up to the Easter Vigil. The presentations of the Creed and Lord's Prayer can be moved to late in the catechumenate if necessary, but the priest, deacon, or DRE should ensure that the catechumens are ready beforehand. If the rites of election and/or calling are celebrated by the bishop elsewhere in the diocese, both the parish and participants will benefit from the *rite of sending*. In this rite, the local pastor and community preliminarily approve and celebrate the participants' readiness (see *RCIA* 106–17, 434–45, 530–46). It demonstrates their present, though distant, love and support and strengthens the catechumens and candidates for their return and entrance into the Lenten season.

The Rite of Election

The rite of election is a major milestone in the catechumens' RCIA journey. Usually occurring on the First Sunday of Lent, catechumens publicly pledge their fidelity to the Church and sign the *Book of the Elect.* Baptized candidates participate in the *rite of calling the candidates to continuing conversion* or in a combined rite. These rites are very similar but do not include any signing.

> The *Journey of Faith* program provides a basic outline to the rite of election in lesson C1 and spiritual preparation through Scripture and reflection in lesson E1: *Election: Saying Yes to Jesus.*

"Before the rite of election the bishop, priests, deacons, catechists, godparents, and the entire community [should] arrive at a judgment about the catechumens' state of formation and progress" (*RCIA* 121). This doesn't mean an interview or exam is needed; however, pastors who have not attended the RCIA sessions may want to speak to you briefly about the group.

This is a good time to gather the team members' and sponsors' feedback and experiences with the catechumens. Recording and sharing particularly meaningful input or stories can serve as a testimony to the individual's faith as well as to the power of the Spirit working in and through your parish RCIA.

The bishop ordinarily admits catechumens and candidates to their respective rites and presides at the ceremony. Whether or not the rite of election is celebrated in your parish, encourage all team members, sponsors, and close family and friends to attend. Prepare the catechumens by reviewing the steps or rehearsing the responses ahead of time. The steps of the rite are listed below.

1. The rite, held within a Mass, begins with the Liturgy of the Word.

2. After the homily, the celebrant calls the catechumens forward by name, along with their godparents.

3. He addresses the assembly and asks the godparents if these men and women are "worthy to be admitted" (*RCIA* 131). He asks if they have "sufficiently prepared…faithfully listened to God's word…[and] responded." The godparents answer, "They have."

4. He asks the catechumens if they wish to enter the Church. They answer, "We do."

5. After their names are signed in the *Book of the Elect*, the celebrant declares that they are members of the elect. He exhorts them to remain faithful and "to reach the fullness of truth" and their godparents to continue their "loving care and example" (*RCIA* 133).

6. The community offers intercessions for the elect.

7. The celebrant prays over the elect and dismisses them before continuing with the Liturgy of the Eucharist.

Sponsors and Godparents: Knowing and Making the Difference

The work of the parish (RCIA) sponsor usually begins during the period of inquiry and continues through the catechumenate. Since the official role ends with the beginning of Lent, the catechumen will choose a *godparent* for baptism. The godparent might be from outside the parish. He or she is ideally someone who has been and will continue to be a Christian model and support for the catechumen through life. It's the godparent's role to present the catechumen at the rite of election and to accompany him or her through the final, intense preparation for initiation. The godparent will also stand with the elect at the celebration of the sacraments and help with his or her continuing Christian formation after Easter. While many parish sponsors serve as godparents, or confirmation sponsors if their candidates are already baptized, all sponsors can continue to offer prayer and support throughout the initiation process and beyond.

Like the sponsor, a godparent must be an active Catholic. Anyone with a preexisting acquaintance is favorable, but the godparent probably should not be a close relative. Godparents should be able to judge the catechumen's progress and faith objectively and challenge him or her in Christian living. This responsibility may interfere with the personal support that naturally comes from family, and not all loved ones feel qualified or prepared. Candidates with eligible baptismal godparents may call on them to be confirmation sponsors. Once a godparent is chosen and approved, invite him or her to the weekly sessions and any preparations for the rites.

Both sponsors and godparents are companions who travel with their participant, represent the Catholic Church, and witness to his or her deepening relationship with Christ. Not everyone travels the same distance or at the same pace, but all learn from each other along the way. The personal connections made through these relationships form and unite the parish and larger Christian community. Encourage them to enjoy the journey.

Effective Catechesis During the Catechumenate

The goal of catechesis in the RCIA is conversion rather than academic or religious mastery. It should be clear, direct, and presented at the participants' level. It must be accurate and promote understanding and acceptance. It must touch their hearts and shine the light of faith on their lives. It must connect to their personal experiences or risk being discarded as irrelevant.

The catechetical model or process of faith formation generally involves three things:

1. *Life experience.*

2. *Message or doctrine.*

3. *Response.*

Personal witness is important in most, if not all, groups that discuss topics of faith, especially the RCIA. As catechists, sponsors, and participants share their stories, they begin to shape a small faith community. They better understand each other's questions, support the personal journeys of others, and reflect on their own.

The sacraments are central to the Christian life and therefore to the *Journey of Faith* catechumenate sessions as well. The images and symbols associated with each sacrament convey scriptural and theological meaning and directly relate to what we do as Catholics. Knowing this is essential to understanding and accepting our faith and will deepen the sacramental and liturgical experiences of all.

The best RCIA program goes beyond the weekly sessions to include private prayer; spiritual reading or study; and acts of charity, justice, or mercy. The process increasingly involves the community of faith, family, and others. As you approach the Easter Vigil, seek out ways in which catechumens and candidates can apply the topics and concepts and witness to their growing faith in both word and action.

Practical Suggestions

- Once participants begin attending Mass or celebrating the word, establish signals and routines that reinforce religious devotion. Sponsors can assist you in modeling proper behaviors until participants have internalized them.

- Make the best use of your materials and resources. Learn the strengths and weaknesses of various formats, media, and types of presentations. Study the *Journey of Faith* content for prayer and activity suggestions. Know when and how to supplement lesson topics, both to individuals and to all participants.

- Learn your catechumens' and candidates' needs and preferences. Continue to leave time for questions and concerns. Adjust the environment and sessions to engage many types of learners and increase understanding. Simple things like prayers, decorations, and refreshments can add interest and a personal touch.

- Connect with spiritual directors in your area. Encourage their services for all participants and make them readily available.

- When presenting the sacraments, allow catechumens to explore and interact with them. Share photos and videos of recent ceremonies. Invite sponsors, clergy, and others to describe their experiences. Compare them to traditions and symbols in other cultures.

- Bring salvation and Church history to life. Show a scene from a modern rendition of an event in the Bible or the life of a saint. Read or distribute short excerpts from magisterial documents. Share an article, press release, or stream a video from a Catholic news source on a current event or relevant topic.

Integrating the Parish Community

For many in the parish, the rites of acceptance and welcoming are a first glimpse into the RCIA process and at the new participants. This increased visibility is a prime opportunity to begin or renew the community's involvement. As the RCIA team and participants develop a rapport and feel more comfortable with the process, continue to seek out ways in which they can interact with their family in faith.

- Ensure that the pastor formally dismisses the RCIA group during Mass from the rite of acceptance until the Easter Vigil. Publicly acknowledging the catechumens' and candidates' presence affirms their dedication and heightens the community's awareness of and appreciation for this ministry. The priest's blessing also strengthens their faith and study.

- During Advent, attend a seasonal prayer service, devotion, or adoration together to expose participants to Catholic traditions.

- Remind parishioners to pray for the catechumens and candidates, to introduce themselves before or after Mass, and to share their faith with others.

- Invite parishioners to attend the weekly sessions and RCIA rites. This better reflects the communal nature of the process and demonstrates the Church's ongoing support.

- Involve team members, sponsors, and ministry members in acquiring supplies, religious objects, and audio and visual aides. Often people have these things already, eliminating the need for a purchase.

- Invite parish ministers and volunteers to speak to the participants, especially if their role or group hasn't been introduced:

  ○ The liturgy committee, music director, sacristans, or wedding coordinator might share how they prepare for Mass, sacraments, and funerals.

  ○ A Bible-study or youth group might provide some information or resources on key Bible passages or events in Church history.

  ○ The pro-life team or St. Vincent de Paul society might give examples of how they are defending human dignity and life and working for justice in the local community. They could also invite participants to contribute or volunteer.

C1: The RCIA Process and Rites

Catechism: 1229–33, 1247–49

Objectives

- Recall the various rites in the RCIA and their respective locations in the process.
- Distinguish between the rites for catechumens and those for baptized candidates, as well between proper (required) and optional rites.
- Realize that participation in each successive rite results in a greater level of commitment and unity for the individual, the parish, and the greater Church.

Leader Meditation

John 1:35–42

Like the prophets before him, John the Baptist pointed the way and prepared individuals to hear and respond to God's invitation to come and follow. While paths and intentions vary from person to person, we can shine light on Christ, the one who reveals who we are and gathers and unites us in his name. Ask Jesus to show you how God is working in your participants and how you can lead them further in the journey of faith.

Related *Catholic Update*

- "Ten Tips for Welcoming New Catholics" (C1202A)

Leader Preparation

- Read the lesson, this lesson plan, the opening Scripture passage, and the *Catechism* sections.
- Read the front sections of this leader guide. Review the *Journey of Faith Inquiry Leader Guide* material as needed, especially that related to lesson *Q1: Welcome to the RCIA!*
- Be familiar with the following vocabulary terms: rite of acceptance, candidate, rite of welcoming, rite of election, elect, scrutinies, presentation of the Creed, presentation of the Lord's Prayer, neophyte. Definitions are provided in this guide's glossary.
- Determine each participant's sacramental status and formation level, if you haven't already. Be prepared to explain the differences between catechumens and candidates and the implications as they relate to the process. Refer to this guide, parish and diocesan policies, or the *rite* itself.
- Obtain copies of any necessary instructions or documentation on your parish's rites of acceptance and welcoming for the participants and sponsors.
- Gather photos or videos of past RCIA rites and/or schedule a former participant or sponsor to share his or her experience(s) during the session.
- Gather extra sheets of paper for the activity, unless you intend to assign this outside of the session or to have participants complete this in their prayer journal. Bringing in some basic art supplies may increase their creativity and make it more meaningful.

Welcome

As the group gathers, welcome the catechumens, candidates, and any new sponsors. Check for supplies and immediate needs. Solicit questions or comments about the previous session and/or share new information and findings. Begin promptly.

Opening Scripture

John 1:35–42

Light the candle and allow for a moment of silence. Then read the passage aloud from a Catholic Bible or study *Lectionary*. Remind participants that this is an account of Jesus' calling his first disciples and that Jesus also calls each of us. Invite them to share any comments or reactions. Ask, "What have you found in Jesus? What have you learned about the Church so far? What more can the RCIA process teach you?"

> From the time of the apostles, becoming a Christian has been accomplished by a journey and initiation in several stages....The catechumenate, or formation of catechumens, aims at bringing their conversion and faith to maturity, in response to the divine initiative and in union with an ecclesial community. *CCC 1229, 1248*

Journey of Faith for Adults, Catechumenate Leader Guide

Journey of Faith

CATECHUMENATE

C1

In Short:
- Each rite in the RCIA includes a period of preparation.
- There are different rites for catechumens and candidates.
- Each rite marks a significant step in the growing commitment to Christ.

The RCIA Process and Rites

You've been exploring what it means to be Catholic—both in your relationship with God and in your life—and you have committed to taking the next step in the RCIA process.

The rites mark significant steps along this RCIA journey. Your RCIA team and sponsor will be by your side, guiding you. Members of the parish will support you through their encouragement and example. And you'll continue to make connections with others who are also traveling this path toward initiation into the Catholic Church.

"As [John the Baptist] watched Jesus walk by, he said, 'Behold, the Lamb of God.' The two disciples heard what he said and followed Jesus. Jesus turned and saw them following him and said to them, 'What are you looking for?' They said to him, 'Rabbi' (which translated means Teacher), 'where are you staying?' He said to them, 'Come, and you will see.'"

John 1:36–39

Periods and Rites

While each person's journey of faith is unique, the Church has established some standard steps marked by rites. Each rite is preceded by a period or stage during which participants receive the formation needed to fully celebrate the coming rite.

The RCIA rites take place at the beginning of Mass or after the homily. You'll stand near the altar with your sponsor and respond to the priest's questions. You may be nervous, so please listen to the words of the prayers as the community prays for you.

- You are on the path of conversion. How have you grown since the beginning of the RCIA process?

Inquiry

As you moved through the inquiry period, you began to follow Jesus more earnestly, came to know his teachings and love more fully, and shared them with others.

Rite: Acceptance

The **rite of acceptance** brings those desiring baptism into the order of catechumens. The rite introduces you to the parish community as members welcome you and pledge their prayers and support. You express your intention to follow the way of Christ, and your sponsor affirms your sincerity and ongoing conversion. As a catechumen, you will continue to grow in faith through study, reflection on the word of God, and prayer.

CCC 1229–1233, 1247–1249

ADULTS

The RCIA Process and Rites

Cite or share examples of personal or cultural rites of passage, and encourage participants to do the same. Point out their similarities, especially to the rites of the RCIA. While their symbolism and actions may differ, their common goal is to express the person's readiness for and acceptance of a new stage in life, with resulting privileges and responsibilities. Explain that the ultimate privilege for Catholics is to fully participate in the sacraments, which promise and prepare us for eternal life.

Periods and Rites

Review the four RCIA periods as needed. Guide participants through the somewhat technical language. A visual chart may help to illustrate the general sequence of rites and distinctions between catechumens and candidates.

Prepare for the rites of acceptance or welcoming, which should quickly follow this session. Give uncatechized participants and inexperienced sponsors enough time and attention to feel comfortable with the process. Display photos or videos of past RCIA rites so they are familiar with common gestures and actions.

Listen to personal testimony from a former RCIA participant, possibly a current team member or a sponsor. Also consider inviting the pastor to share his experience and perspective as a celebrating minister.

Inquiry

Ask participants how many are unbaptized or baptized.

Emphasize that the separate rites aren't to exclude but to eventually unite everyone in the same sacraments.

Baptism will be discussed in more detail in lesson C3, but if participants have questions about why those baptized in another faith tradition do not have to be rebaptized in the Catholic Church, you can refer them to the section of the *Catechism* on baptism which starts at *CCC* 1213. You can also cite Ephesians 4:5, "one Lord, one faith, one baptism."

Alot time at the end of your lesson for a personal testimony from a former RCIA participant.

---

1. As the rite begins, you may stand at the church doors to symbolize your desire to enter the community.
2. The priest introduces you by name to those gathered and asks, "What do you ask of the Church?" You answer, "Faith," indicating your intention to live, learn, and love according to Christ's call and example.
3. The priest asks your sponsor to accept his or her role and then marks the sign of the cross on your forehead, symbolizing the love and strength of Christ that accompanies you. (An optional signing of other senses includes ears, eyes, lips, heart, shoulders, hands, and feet.)
4. The priest formally invites you to enter the church and participate in the Liturgy of the Word. (After the petitions, the RCIA group may be dismissed to reflect more deeply on the word of God.)

Rite: Welcoming
If you're already baptized, you enter the catechumenate period as a **candidate** through the **rite of welcoming**. This rite may be celebrated separately or may be combined with the rite of acceptance.

- Who or what is helping you as you make this journey?
- In what specific ways are you growing in your relationship with Christ?

Catechumenate

The catechumenate period is a time of focused learning on topics related to Catholic belief and practice, training you in the Christian life. It is a time of "more intense preparation for the sacraments of initiation" (RCIA chapter of *The Rites, Volume One* [RCIA], 6).

"[Jesus] saw a tax collector named Levi sitting at the customs post. He said to him, 'Follow me.' And leaving everything behind, he got up and followed him."

Luke 5:27–28

Rite: Election
Your parish may have a rite of sending to offer their prayers and support as you prepare to travel to your diocesan cathedral for the rite of election. During the rite of election you'll be presented to the bishop or his delegate.

The **rite of election**, usually celebrated on the first Sunday of Lent, affirms your readiness for the sacraments of initiation. You become a member of the **elect**, indicating you have been chosen—elected—by God and the Church. During the rite of election:

1. Your godparent(s) affirm your readiness, and the worshiping community voices its approval.
2. The celebrant asks if you wish to enter the Church. With the other catechumens, you answer, "We do."

Journey of Faith for Adults, Catechumenate Leader Guide

3. At either the rite of sending or the rite of election, you sign your name in the *Book of the Elect*, expressing your "wish to enter fully into the life of the Church through the sacraments of baptism, confirmation, and the Eucharist" at Easter (*RCIA* 553).

4. The community prays for the elect, and the bishop offers a special blessing.

If you are already baptized, you will celebrate a rite named the call to continuing conversion.

> *"Do not fear, for I have redeemed you; I have called you by name: you are mine."*
>
> Isaiah 43:1

Purification and Enlightenment

Usually coinciding with the season of Lent, this period is a time of reflection that focuses on your conversion as one of the elect, preparing to celebrate the Easter sacraments. Minor rites—such as the **scrutinies**, **presentation of the Creed**, and **presentation of the Lord's Prayer**—occur during this time, often at Sunday Mass.

> *"Jesus said to his disciples, "Whoever wishes to come after me must deny himself, take up his cross, and follow me.""*
>
> Matthew 16:24

Rites: Sacraments of Initiation

The Easter Vigil Mass is the "holy night," the "truly blessed night," the "night of grace" (The Easter Proclamation [*Exsultet*], *The Roman Missal*). The Church keeps vigil for the resurrection of Jesus and celebrates the central mysteries of our faith.

The elect are fully initiated into the Catholic Church at the Easter Vigil Mass through reception of the sacraments of initiation. You will be baptized, sealed with the gift of the Holy Spirit in confirmation, and receive Eucharist for the first time. From this point, if you are newly baptized, you will be called a **neophyte** (Greek for "newly planted"). If you have already been baptized, you will make a profession of faith and celebrate confirmation and Eucharist.

> *"This is the night, when Christ broke the prison-bars of death and rose victorious from the underworld."*
>
> The Easter Proclamation [*Exsultet*], *The Roman Missal*

Mystagogy

Initiation isn't the end; it begins your new life and the period of mystagogy. During the Easter season, you will experience being a full member of the Catholic Christian community. You will participate in the Sunday Eucharist and reflect on the meaning of the Easter sacraments.

- What part of, or moment in, this process interests you most? Why?

The RCIA Process and Rites

Your Journey of Faith

Consider assigning this activity to team members and sponsors ahead of time so they may share their timelines with participants during the session.

Distribute any extra paper or supplies as you introduce the activity. Encourage them to express their experiences in any way or form they desire. It may be beneficial, more effective, or simply necessary to have participants complete this on their own. If so, invite them to share some highlights and milestones at the next session.

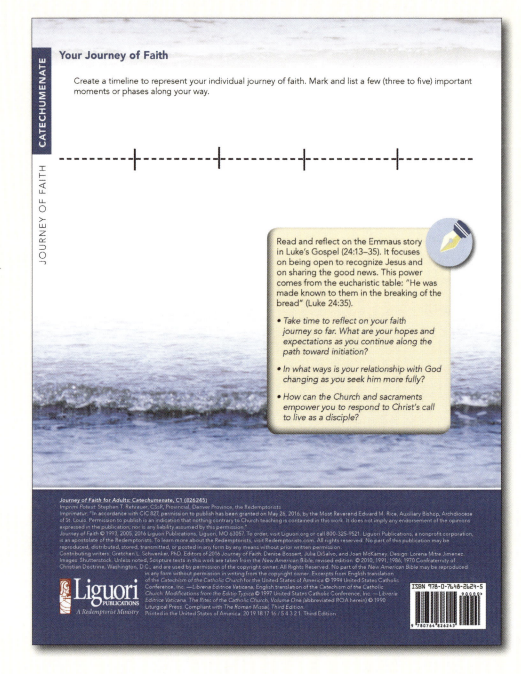

Journey of Faith for Adults, Catechumenate Leader Guide

Journaling

Encourage participants to share their responses with their sponsor this week.

Closing Prayer

Solicit special intentions from all those present, then pray the *Our Father* together. Remind participants that this prayer proclaims oneness in God, faithfulness to his will, and frequent nourishment as he leads us along the path of faith.

Take-home

Send participants and sponsors home with a list of key dates or a general calendar of RCIA events, if they don't have this information already. Encourage them to add these details to their personal, family, or digital calendars. Remind them of any necessary preparations for the rite of acceptance and/or welcoming and to look forward to the process that culminates in the sacraments of initiation. Leaders and team members should consider making cards or planning a small celebration for those formally entering the catechumenate.

The RCIA Process and Rites

C2: The Sacraments: An Introduction

Catechism: 1084, 1087, 1113–34, 1210–12, 1420–21, 1533–35

Objectives

Participants will…

- describe a sacrament as a tangible sign and manifestation of divine love and presence.
- distinguish between the seven sacraments of the Church and other divine encounters.
- classify the sacraments according to the *Catechism*'s categories of Initiation, Healing, and Service.
- identify Christ as instituting the sacraments and the Church as their proper minister.

Leader Meditation

Matthew 28:16–20

Jesus promises, "I am with you always, until the end of the age." Through the sacraments, the Lord is visibly present in the Church and in our lives. Each sacrament we receive increases both the Lord's presence and our own awareness of that presence. Ask yourself, "What makes the sacraments unique? How do I value them in my daily life?"

Related *Catholic Updates*

- "Sacraments: It All Starts with Jesus" (C9308A)
- "Sacraments of Initiation: God's 'I Love You'" (C0904A)
- "What Are Sacraments?" (C9508A)

Leader Preparation

- Read the lesson, this lesson plan, the opening Scripture, and the *Catechism* sections.
- Be familiar with the following vocabulary terms: sacrament, grace. Definitions are provided in the lesson as well as in this guide's glossary.
- Be aware that catechumens do not receive the sacraments in the same sequence as cradle Catholics, and that candidates may have experienced or may perceive certain sacraments in a different way.
- Invite the hospitality team to do something special that fits with this lesson's message. Flowers, candy, or other inexpensive gifts would demonstrate that outward signs *really do* express invisible realities—like the parish's ongoing support and care.

Welcome

Greet the participants and sponsors as they gather. Check for supplies and immediate needs. Invite each person to share one event on his or her timeline of faith, if this activity was not completed during the previous session. Then invite them to share their experiences of and reactions to the rite of acceptance and/or welcoming. Begin promptly.

Opening Scripture

Matthew 28:16–20

Light the candle and read the passage aloud. Ask the participants to name ways that Jesus is with us, both individually and as a Church. Explain that the sacraments are the unique and ultimate means by which Christ's grace and saving actions enter our lives and strengthen our faith. Their visible and tangible signs serve as proof of God's eternal love and presence.

> Sacraments are "powers that come forth" from the body of Christ, which is ever-living and life-giving. They are actions of the Holy Spirit at work in his body, the Church.
>
> *CCC 1116*

Journey of Faith for Adults, Catechumenate Leader Guide

Journey of Faith

C2 · CATECHUMENATE · ADULTS

In Short:
- A sacrament is a visible sign of God's grace.
- The seven sacraments fall into three categories.
- Christ instituted the sacraments and made the Church their minister.

The Sacraments: An Introduction

How do you communicate your love to someone? We're physical beings living in a physical world, so we communicate in physical ways. We experience life through our senses, and we communicate through our senses, too.

We can experience love, and love is real, but it's not a physical object. Our expressions of love aren't the same as love, but we communicate our love through them. Words, gestures, and physical objects become signs of our love.

Jesus realized that as physical beings, we need physical signs to comprehend the incredible reality of his love. When Christ uses physical signs—symbols we can sense and observe—to work in us, the Church calls it a **sacrament**.

The following Scripture readings will show you a few of the ways Jesus used the physical world to help his followers understand his profound love for them. As you read, list the way each reading shows this.

Matthew 8:1–3   Mark 10:13–16
Luke 9:12–17   John 9:6–7
John 11:35–36   John 13:4–5
John 20:21–22

What Is a Sacrament?

In the broadest sense, a sacrament can be any person, event, or thing through which we encounter or experience God's presence in a new or deeper way. A sunset, a period of quiet prayer, a storm, the birth of a child, an intimate conversation with a close friend—all have the potential for revealing God to us in new and deeper ways.

In the broad sense, then, we can say that a sacramental experience is an encounter with God through human experience that somehow changes us. Virtually any human experience can provide us with such an encounter.

CCC 1084, 1087, 1113–34, 1210–12, 1420–21, 1533–35

How Does Jesus Communicate Love?

Share these responses with participants as needed:

- Matthew 8:1–3 "[Jesus] stretched out his hand, touched him, and said, 'I will do it. Be made clean.'" Christ used the laying on of hands and words of invocation to manifest healing.
- Mark 10:13–16 "Then he embraced them and blessed them, placing his hands on them." Jesus welcomed children into fellowship and blessed them through physical touch and embrace.
- Luke 9:12–17 "Then taking the five loaves and the two fish, and looking up to heaven, he said the blessing over them, broke them, and gave them to the disciples…" Jesus multiplied food and fed a crowd using prayer and the distribution of material gifts. This directly correlates to the Eucharist.
- John 9:6–7 "[Jesus] spat on the ground and made clay with the saliva, and smeared the clay on his eyes, and said to him, 'Go wash…' So he went and washed, and came back able to see." Jesus effected healing and restored sight through a physical washing with water.
- John 11:35–36 "And Jesus wept." Jesus demonstrated his love for his friends (us) through natural human emotions.
- John 13:4–5 "[Jesus] took a towel and tied it around his waist. Then he poured water into a basin and began to wash the disciples' feet…" Jesus physically demonstrated his servant leadership in this act. In his time, one might offer water for washing as a sign of hospitality or welcome, but to wash others was a sign of humility, even servitude. It also may represent purification.
- John 20:21–22 "[Jesus] breathed on them and said to them, 'Receive the holy Spirit.'" The Holy Spirit is often conveyed as breath or wind. It recalls the breath and wind of life present in creation (Genesis 1:2, 2:7).

Clarify the meanings of *sign* and *symbol*. Begin with familiar examples, perhaps asking participants for a few. For instance, road signs help us navigate through a complex traffic system. However, simply putting up a sign won't create a lane or intersection—worse, putting up the *wrong* sign could cause confusion or injury. The sign must clearly and accurately convey the underlying truth. *This role of signs and symbols in our pursuit of knowledge and truth is of great importance.*

The Sacraments: An Introduction

Sacraments Are Expressions of God's Grace

Explain that "Grace is a *participation in the life of God*" (*CCC* 1997). The *Catechism* describes different types of grace (*CCC* 1996–2005): *sanctifying grace*, sometimes called *justifying* or *habitual grace*, which is necessary for heaven; *actual graces*, which are individual acts of God that help and strengthen us; *sacramental graces*, "gifts proper to the different sacraments"; and *special graces*, or *charisms*, which serve the common good and benefit the whole Church (*CCC* 2003, 799–801).

Sacraments Are Expressions of God's Grace

In the fifth century, St. Augustine defined *sacrament* as "a visible sign of invisible grace." To understand sacrament, we also need to understand what **grace** means. Grace is the gift of God's love and presence into which we grow. It's "the help God gives us to respond to our vocation to become his adopted sons and daughters." God's "initiative of grace precedes, prepares, and elicits our free response in faith and commitment" (*United States Catholic Catechism for Adults*, glossary, p. 514).

Grace is a relationship between God and us. Our side of the relationship develops gradually, but it's a response to a love that was always there. The gift of God's grace is totally free and ever present. What we do with that gift is ours to choose, and our eternal salvation is affected by our choice. We express and celebrate our acceptance of it in the sacraments.

- Reflect on a way God has loved you through another person, a specific event, or physical object.
- Give an example of how God has used you to show his love to others.

Jesus as Sacrament

Those who first followed Jesus encountered God and God's presence in a new way through his human presence. Jesus was, for them—and is for us—*the* sacrament of God. In Jesus, we encounter God and God's presence. Jesus is the one great sacrament through which all other sacraments make sense.

"In the beginning was the Word, and the Word was with God, and the Word was God. And the Word became flesh and made his dwelling among us, and we saw his glory, the glory as of the Father's only Son, full of grace and truth."

John 1:1, 14

- How have you encountered God's presence and love for you through Jesus?

The Church as Sacrament

In reflecting on this special relationship, the Church discovered its unique vocation: just as Jesus used his physical body to carry out the Father's mission, the Church uses its human members (the Mystical Body) as an instrument of salvation—as "sacraments" for the world. Sacraments are physical expressions of spiritual realities. As the body of Christ on earth, the Church is called to be a physical sign of the spiritual reality of Christ's ongoing presence in the world.

- How is your local parish community a sign of Christ's love to others?

What Are the Seven Sacraments?

The official seven sacraments of the Catholic Church are baptism, confirmation, Eucharist, penance and reconciliation, anointing of the sick, matrimony, and holy orders. They are commonly grouped under three headings:

Sacraments of Initiation
These sacraments celebrate and introduce us to the experience of the Christian life. While most Catholics receive these in separate ceremonies over several years, catechumens are initiated in one combined rite at the Easter Vigil.

What Are the Seven Sacraments?

Review the groupings of sacraments and point out that they will be presented in that order: first initiation, then healing, and finally service. The symbols, ritual steps, and meanings of each sacrament can be found in the next lessons (C3–9).

Mention that each sacrament has a proper *matter* and *form* (material and action; a quick chart could be shared). While they cannot fully contain the mysteries they hold, they are the *necessary means* by which the effects become present (for example, without water, there is no baptism). Conversely, the next lesson (C3: *The Sacrament of Baptism*) explains why Christian candidates are not "rebaptized"—it's impossible to undo or redo divine work.

Journey of Faith for Adults, Catechumenate Leader Guide

- *Baptism* incorporates us into the Church and gives us a rebirth as daughters and sons of God.

- *Confirmation* is a continuation, ratification, or sealing of baptism. It helps us focus on the missionary dimensions of the baptismal commitment.

- *Eucharist* is the preeminent sacrament from which all others have meaning. In the Eucharist, Christ is most profoundly present in the Church, which gathers to hear the word of God and to share the nourishment of Christ's Body with one another.

Sacraments of Healing

These sacraments celebrate and reveal to us God's power to heal us in soul and body.

- *Penance and reconciliation* focuses on forgiveness in our lives and on our acceptance of that forgiveness, which brings us back to spiritual health in the family of God after we have turned away.

- *Anointing of the sick* takes place as representatives of the community gather in faith to pray over and lay hands on those who are sick. The Church, like Christ, desires the health of the whole human person.

Sacraments of Service

These sacraments celebrate the Christian vocation of service and consecrate us to minister within our own families and within the wider Church community.

- *Matrimony* (marriage) celebrates and witnesses the covenant of love between two people and symbolizes in that union Christ's covenant of love for the Church.

- *Holy orders* (ordination) is a sacrament of service by which some are called by God, through the Church, to be spiritual leaders.

You will learn more about each of the sacraments as you continue your study.

How Do the Sacraments "Work?"

The traditional explanation is that the sacraments *effect*, or bring about, what they symbolize. For example, the pouring of or immersion into water in the rite of baptism symbolizes the soul being cleansed of sin. At the same time, God is making that cleansing happen. The laying on of hands and anointing in the rite of confirmation *both symbolize and make happen* the sealing of the recipient with the gift of the Holy Spirit. This occurs "independently of the personal holiness of the minister....The fruits of the sacraments also depend on the disposition of the one who receives them" (*CCC* 1128).

Sacraments Celebrate Christ's Life

The Church teaches that the seven sacraments were instituted by Christ. The sacraments come out of the story of Jesus' life and actions. For example, baptism calls to mind the baptism of Jesus in the Jordan and the way Jesus gathered a community around himself. It also reminds us of Jesus' command to carry the gospel to others and to baptize them. The Eucharist recalls the Last Supper. The Gospels also include accounts of other meals when Jesus invited those who were rejected by others to eat with him. Penance and reconciliation reminds us of Jesus' invitation to forgive one another, and of the way he forgave those who put him to death.

The sacraments also flow from Jesus' values and teachings. He raised basic values and experiences (forgiveness, concern for the sick, marriage, service) to new levels. He transformed ordinary human values into spiritual values by helping people see God's love made visible through them. As we celebrate the sacraments, we, like the first followers of Jesus, have the opportunity to encounter him in our acceptance of the values he lived and affirmed. In that encounter, Jesus is present to us as he was present to the early Church.

When Jesus instituted the sacraments and placed Peter at the head of the Church, he gave the apostles, and those who follow them in leading the Church, the mission and authority to minister and maintain the sacraments.

How Do the Sacraments "Work?"

Distinguish between sacramental grace and superstition (*CCC* 2110–11, 2138).

Offer simple, straightforward responses if participants express concerns surrounding sacramental doctrine and practice. Refer them to the pastor if complex or pastoral matters are raised.

Sacraments Celebrate the Community's Life

Ask participants for examples of personal, social, or cultural rituals, such as birthday, wedding, and holiday traditions. Then ask, "What good do these acts and events maintain within your family or community?" Explain that the sacraments have the same function and purpose.

Ask the participants, "What attracts you to the Church's sacraments? What benefits do you see to having each of the seven sacraments?"

Invite candidates, sponsors, or leaders to share their experiences with the sacraments (for instance, baptism, Eucharist, marriage).

The Sacraments: An Introduction

Share these responses to Jesus' signs of love as needed:

- Mark 14:3–9 "A woman came with an alabaster jar of perfumed oil, costly genuine spikenard. She broke the alabaster jar and poured it on his head....Jesus said, '…She has done a good thing for me.'"
  The woman, aware of Jesus' impending death, responded to his loving sacrifice by preparing his body for burial.

- Luke 7:36–39 "[The sinful woman] stood behind [Jesus] at his feet weeping and began to bathe his feet with her tears. Then she wiped them with her hair, kissed them, and anointed them with the ointment."
  This woman responded to Christ's forgiveness and mercy with a (physical) sign of love.

- Luke 10:38–42 "She had a sister named Mary [who] sat beside the Lord at his feet listening to him speak. Martha, burdened with much serving, came to him....The Lord said to her in reply, '…Mary has chosen the better part…'"
  Both sisters responded to Jesus' presence and friendship: Martha with hospitality, Mary with fellowship and devotion.

- Luke 5:27–32 "And leaving everything behind, he got up and followed him. Then Levi gave a great banquet for him in his house…"
  Levi (Matthew) responded to Christ's invitation with a total life change, discipleship, and celebration.

CATECHUMENATE

JOURNEY OF FAITH

Sacraments Celebrate the Life of the Community

Each sacrament celebrates through ritual and symbols something happening in the lives of the celebrating community. For example, Eucharist strengthens the unity of Christians as they receive it. It celebrates God's nourishing presence with us now.

While the sacraments benefit us as individuals, they also bring life to the entire Church. As members of Christ's body, when we are strengthened as individuals, the family of God is strengthened as a whole (CCC 1134). Sacraments are more than just one-time liturgical celebrations. They serve as ongoing symbols of God's love made visible to and through us.

Looking for and responding to Jesus' signs of love will keep our connection to God alive and strong. Read about some of the ways people in the Bible responded to Jesus' signs of love. Discuss what you find with the rest of the group.

Mark 14:3–9	Luke 7:36–39
Luke 10:38–42	Luke 5:27–32

- *When you experience God's love, how do you respond?*

Reflect on the question below in your prayer journal:

- *How might the sacraments help keep my heart open to God's love?*

Journey of Faith for Adults: Catechumenate, C2 (826245)
Imprimi Potest: Stephen T. Rehrauer, CSsR, Provincial, Denver Province, the Redemptorists.
Imprimatur: "In accordance with CIC 827, permission to publish has been granted on May 26, 2016, by the Most Reverend Edward M. Rice, Auxiliary Bishop, Archdiocese of St. Louis. Permission to publish is an indication that nothing contrary to Church teaching is contained in this work. It does not imply any endorsement of the opinions expressed in the publication; nor is any liability assumed by this permission."
Journey of Faith © 1993, 2005, 2016 Liguori Publications, Liguori, MO 63057. To order, visit Liguori.org or call 800-325-9521. Liguori Publications, a nonprofit corporation, is an apostolate of the Redemptorists. To learn more about the Redemptorists, visit Redemptorists.com. All rights reserved. No part of this publication may be reproduced, distributed, stored, transmitted, or posted in any form by any means without prior written permission.
Contributing writers: Fr. Patrick Kaler, CSsR; Fr. Michael Henesy, CSsR; Terry Matz; Sandra DeGidio, OSM; and Joseph Martos. Editors of 2016 Journey of Faith: Denise Bossert, Julia DiSalvo, and Joan McKamey. Design: Lorena Mitre Jimenez. Images: Shutterstock. Unless noted, Scripture texts in this work are taken from the *New American Bible*, revised edition © 2010, 1991, 1986, 1970 Confraternity of Christian Doctrine, Washington, D.C., and are used by permission of the copyright owner. All Rights Reserved. No part of the *New American Bible* may be reproduced in any form without permission in writing from the copyright owner. Excerpts from English translation of the *Catechism of the Catholic Church* for the United States of America © 1994 United States Catholic Conference, Inc. —Libreria Editrice Vaticana; English translation of the *Catechism of the Catholic Church: Modifications from the Editio Typica* © 1997 United States Catholic Conference, Inc. —Libreria Editrice Vaticana. *United States Catholic Catechism for Adults* © 2006 U.S. Conference of Catholic Bishops; all rights reserved. Compliant with *The Roman Missal, Third Edition*. Printed in the United States of America. 20 19 18 17 16 / 5 4 3 2 1. Third Edition.

Liguori PUBLICATIONS
A Redemptorist Ministry

Journaling

Encourage participants to reflect on the question throughout the week. Remind them to seek inspiration and ideas from Scripture, which is full of people who experienced and responded to God's love (see lesson activity).

Closing Prayer

Request special intentions from the group, then pray the Glory Be (Doxology). This simple prayer proclaims God's faithful presence in our lives—yesterday, today, and tomorrow.

Looking Ahead

The next lesson, *C3: The Sacrament of Baptism*, focuses on the first and fundamental sacrament, which begins our life in Christ. Have each participant talk with his or her sponsor or another parishioner about why the sacramental life of the Church is such a blessing.

The Sacraments: An Introduction

C3: The Sacrament of Baptism

Catechism: 1212–84

Objectives

Participants will…

- identify baptism as necessary for salvation and for membership in the Church.
- recognize that baptism is the beginning of our life (of grace) in Christ and the washing away of the old person, of sin, and of the power of death.
- draw parallels between the signs of baptism, their biblical significance, and their worldly significancce.

Leader Meditation

Mark 1:4–11

Most Catholics can't recall their own baptisms. Yet many times along our journey, we review and remake the promises made for us by our parents and godparents. Renew your baptismal promises now and pray for the grace and strength to become all for which God has created you.

Related *Catholic Updates*

- "The Sacrament of Baptism: Celebrating the Embrace of God" (C8903A)
- "Sacraments of Initiation, Sacraments of Invitation" (C0103A)

Leader Preparation

- Read the lesson, this lesson plan, the opening Scripture, and the *Catechism* sections.
- Be familiar with the following vocabulary terms: baptism, original sin, chrism. Definitions are provided in this guide's glossary.
- Obtain a copy of the baptismal promises to reflect upon during the closing prayer.

Welcome

Greet each person as he or she arrives. Check for supplies and immediate needs. Solicit questions or comments about the previous session and/or share new information and findings. Begin promptly.

Opening Scripture

Mark 1:4–11

Light the candle and read the passage aloud. Allow for a moment of silence, then point out that even Jesus accepted baptism by and within the faith community. You may also mention that his presentation in the Temple as an infant (Luke 2:22–38) similarly reflects his adherence to religious tradition. Ask the participants, "How might this reflect the necessity of baptism? What makes this sacrament special?"

> The faith required for baptism is not a perfect and mature faith, but a beginning that is called to develop. The catechumen or the godparent is asked: "What do you ask of God's Church?" The response is: Faith. *CCC 1253*

Journey of Faith for Adults, Catechumenate Leader Guide

C3 CATECHUMENATE

In Short:
- Baptism is our entry into the body of Christ and family of God.
- Through baptism, we die to sin and rise to new life in Christ.
- Signs of the rite include water, oil, a white garment, and a lighted candle.

- How would your life change if you died to sin and lived for Christ.

The Sacrament of Baptism

The word baptism means "plunging." At our **baptism** we plunge into the death and resurrection of Christ. Jesus called his death and resurrection a baptism: "There is a baptism with which I must be baptized, and how great is my anguish until it is accomplished!" (Luke 12:50).

This is the double action of our redemption: Christ *going down into the grave* for our sins and *rising again*, glorious, triumphant, immortal. Through baptism, Christians are united with his saving death and life-giving resurrection.

Saint Paul emphasizes that baptism is the beginning of a vital union with the risen Lord. The old sinful self passes away to be born anew and conformed to Christ.

Read the following passages and reflect on what they say about being buried with Christ, dying to sin, and rising to new life in Christ:

Romans 6:4 Romans 6:6–7
Romans 6:9–11

Baptized Into the Body of Christ

For Christians, community has always been an essential part of life. Christ is at the center, and the community is built around him. Baptism is the way we enter that community and become members of the body of Christ, the Church. Once baptized, we share in the privileges and life of this community of believers.

Many people think of baptism as a private family affair, but being baptized connects us in a deep and eternal way with a much larger family: the family of God.

Heirs of God's Kingdom

Baptism is the sign of salvation given to us by Christ to bring us into the kingdom of God (see John 3:5). A person enters "into Christ" (Romans 6:3, Galatians 3:27) at the time of baptism, and the gift of the Spirit is given at that time.

"We are children of God, and if children, then heirs, heirs of God and joint heirs with Christ, if only we suffer with him so that we may also be glorified with him."

Romans 8:16–18

As adopted sons and daughters of God, Christians share in Jesus' own relationship with his Father—a relationship so intimate that they, like Jesus, can freely and with every confidence address the Lord of heaven as "Father."

CCC 1212–84

ADULTS

Baptized Into the Body of Christ

Emphasize that baptism involves the community of believers as well as the person being baptized.

Does a Protestant Have to Be Rebaptized in the Catholic Church?

Remind participants, if necessary, why a Christian is never baptized more than once: Ultimately, the effects of the sacrament's divine work can never be undone and therefore remain (see lesson C2). Explain that baptized Catholics who wish to return to active participation need only to receive the sacrament of penance, then if necessary, complete their initiation by requesting Eucharist and confirmation (sometimes through the RCIA).

Involve the pastor whenever there is a question of baptismal validity. Any participant whose baptismal ceremony or form is in question may have the option of receiving (valid) baptism in a private ceremony prior to the Easter Vigil (*National Statutes for the Catechumenate*, 37; Canon 869).

The Sacrament of Baptism

Give participants time to complete the activity in this section on their own. Then discuss as a group. *Share these responses with participants as needed:*

- Romans 6:4 "We were indeed buried with him through baptism into death, so that, just as Christ was raised from the dead by the glory of the Father, we too might live in newness of life."
Baptism is a spiritual death or burial to sin and rising to faith and grace (salvation).

- Romans 6:6–7 "We know that our old self was crucified with him, so that our sinful body might be done away with, that we might no longer be in slavery to sin."
In baptism, we unite our fallen selves to Christ's crucifixion, which redeems us from all sin.

- Romans 6:9–11 "[Christ] died to sin once and for all; as to his life, he lives for God. Consequently, you too must think of yourselves as [being] dead to sin and living for God…"
Baptism calls us, and empowers us, to Christian discipleship and a life of virtue.

The Sacrament of Baptism

What Happens During the Rite of Baptism?

Discuss the symbols and gestures connected to baptism: the sacred chrism, the white garment, the Easter candle, the pouring of or immersion into water, the words *I baptize you in the name of the Father....* Review their meanings and emphasize their significance. Ask, "Why is water the perfect symbol of new life? How might these symbols and gestures—and the sacrament itself—be a source of hope?"

Why Water?

Explain the meaning of *original sin* (CCC 416–18). Make sure the participants understand original sin as it relates to their lives: Put simply, our human nature makes us imperfect.

Discuss the important of water in the sacrament of baptism. Why is water the perfect symbol of new life?

Suggested responses include: Water is symbolic of the cleansing that takes place during baptism. Christ washes us free from sin and, through baptism, both original sin and all our personal sins are washed away.

You may also want to discuss the importance of the sign (the pouring of water or the immersion into water) and the words, "I baptize you in the name of the Father..."

Suggested responses include: The pouring or immersion reminds us that our sins are being washed away. Through the invocation of the Holy Trinity the Church "asks God that through his Son the power of the Holy Spirit may be sent upon the water" (CCC 1239). The importance of the Trinity can be emphasized by pouring water over the baptized three times, or submerging him or her in water three times.

- As a child and heir of God, what riches will you inherit through baptism?
- What responsibilities come with those riches?

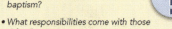

Does a Protestant Have to Be Rebaptized in the Catholic Church?

The short answer is no. The *Rite of Christian Initiation of Adults* explains, "Baptism is a sacramental bond of unity linking all who have been signed by it. Because of that unchangeable effect,...the rite of baptism is held in highest honor by all Christians. Once it has been validly celebrated, even if by Christians with whom we are not in full communion, it may never lawfully be repeated" (*The Rites, Volume One, General Introduction, [RCIA]*, 4). Protestants wishing to join the Catholic Church are only rebaptized if there's significant doubt that they were baptized.

Baptism confers the character of Christ, making it permanent and irrevocable. As St. Paul wrote, there is "one Lord, one faith, one baptism; one God and Father of all, who is over all and through all and in all" (Ephesians 4:1–6).

What Happens to People Who Aren't Baptized?

Catholics believe that God's mercy can supply for the lack of baptism in a way that hasn't been revealed. Catholics believe that children who aren't baptized are entrusted to the infinitely kind and powerful love of God who wants all his children to be with him in heaven. Some people once held the theory that infants who die without baptism were excluded from heaven but spent eternity in a state of natural happiness called *limbo*. This theory has never been explicitly taught by the Church.

Catholics also believe in:

- "baptism of blood" (suffering death for the Christian faith before baptism)
- "baptism of desire" (those who "through no fault of their own do not know the gospel of Christ or his Church, yet sincerely seek God and moved by grace, strive by their deeds to do his will as it is known to them through the dictates of conscience," (Dogmatic Constitution on the Church [*Lumen Gentium*], 16).

What Happens During the Rite of Baptism?

The sacraments don't just tell us about something. They make the event happen. They are signs that work—that have effect. The sign accomplishes what it signifies.

In baptism, the essential sign is the pouring of water three times on the person's head or the immersion of the candidate in water three times accompanied by the words: "I baptize you in the name of the Father, and of the Son, and of the Holy Spirit."

Why Water?

We know the importance of water for *life*. We know, too, that a person can live for weeks without food but only a few days without water to drink. Water is the main element that makes up living tissue—as much as 99 percent. No wonder our Lord chose water to represent the beginning of the new Christian life.

But water can remind us of *death* as well (flooding, drowning). This is another reason why our Lord chose water to represent the end of the old life and the beginning of the new Christian life.

The waters of baptism remind us that Christ has *washed us clean of sin* and reconciled us with God. In baptism, all our sins—even original sin, the fallen state of all human beings—are washed away. That's why the baptismal promises include renunciation of sin and a profession of personal faith.

Journey of Faith for Adults, Catechumenate Leader Guide

Anointing, White Garment, and Lighted Candle

If baptism is celebrated separate from confirmation, as is the case with infants and young children, the minister anoints the newly baptized with **chrism**, olive oil mixed with balsam and consecrated by the bishop. This anointing is a sign that God has "put his seal upon us and given the Spirit in our hearts as a first installment" (2 Corinthians 1:22). It's a sign that the baptized person shares in the kingly, prophetic, and priestly mission of Christ.

After the water bath of baptism, the minister presents a white garment and a candle to the newly baptized. The *white garment* symbolizes becoming a new creation and being clothed in Christ: "For all of you who were baptized into Christ have clothed yourselves with Christ" (Galatians 3:27).

The candle is lit from the Easter candle, which represents the risen Christ. The *lighted candle* is a reminder that Christ, the light of the world, is their light and that they must "live as children of light" (Ephesians 5:8).

A Short History of Baptism

Bloody persecutions and heresies (false teachings) threatened new converts, especially those poorly instructed in the faith. The Church established the catechumenate, an extended period of preparation (sometimes lasting three or more years) to make sure candidates were sincere and well-grounded in the faith before baptism.

When Emperor Constantine embraced Christianity in AD 313, large numbers of people entered the Church. To adjust to these numbers, the Church began to drop the long catechumenate.

Until recently, adults interested in joining the Catholic Church received private instruction from a priest. After World War II, the Church in Africa addressed the need for more preparation for its new members by reviving the ancient catechumenate process.

The Second Vatican Council (1962–65) called for the restoration of the ancient catechumenate process for the whole Church. The *Rite of Christian Initiation of Adults* became mandatory in the United States in 1988. RCIA helps prepare those interested in joining the Catholic Church to follow Christ and integrates them into the life of the Church community.

Baptism is "the door to life and to the kingdom of God."

RCIA, General Introduction, 3

Why Does the Church Baptize Infants?

The New Testament refers to entire households being baptized—and the Greek word for "household" includes everyone from infant to the oldest members of the family (see Acts 16:33; 1 Corinthians 1:16). By the second century, St. Irenaeus considered it a matter of course that infants and small children, as well as adults, should be baptized. The Church considers Jesus' invitation to baptism to be an invitation of universal and limitless love, which applies to children as well as to adults.

"To fulfill the true meaning of the sacrament, children must later be formed in the faith in which they have been baptized...so that they may ultimately accept for themselves the faith in which they have been baptized."

Rite of Baptism for Children

Anointing, White Garment, and Lighted Candle

Discuss the meaning and importance of the sacred chrism, the white garment, and the Easter candle.

Suggested responses include: The sacred chrism becomes the physical sign of the gift of the Holy Spirit; the white garment symbolizes that the newly baptized have "put on Christ" and risen with Christ; the Easter candle symbolizes the light of Christ in the world and the newly baptized's call to go out and be a light to the world.

Explain that *chrism* is only one of three blessed or holy oils. Each year at the chrism Mass on Holy Thursday, the bishop blesses these oils to be distributed and used among the parishes:

- *oil of catechumens* (before baptism)
- *(sacred) chrism* (after baptism) — olive oil mixed with balsam
- *oil of the sick* — used in the sacrament of anointing of the sick

The Sacrament of Baptism

Baptism Is a Beginning

Emphasize that although baptism is a culmination of the RCIA process, it is truly a new beginning in each catechumen's life of faith. As Christians, our formation, conversion, and growth in virtue are ongoing and lifelong.

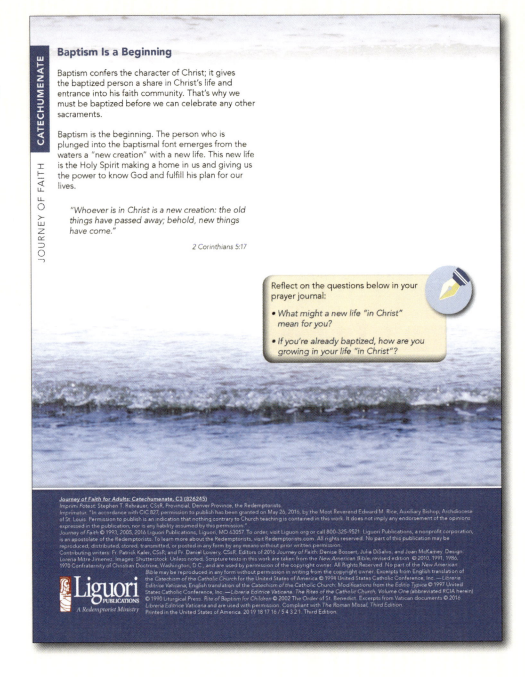

Baptism Is a Beginning

Baptism confers the character of Christ; it gives the baptized person a share in Christ's life and entrance into his faith community. That's why we must be baptized before we can celebrate any other sacraments.

Baptism is the beginning. The person who is plunged into the baptismal font emerges from the waters a "new creation" with a new life. This new life is the Holy Spirit making a home in us and giving us the power to know God and fulfill his plan for our lives.

"Whoever is in Christ is a new creation: the old things have passed away; behold, new things have come."

2 Corinthians 5:17

Reflect on the questions below in your prayer journal:
- What might a new life "in Christ" mean for you?
- If you're already baptized, how are you growing in your life "in Christ"?

Journey of Faith for Adults, Catechumenate Leader Guide

Journaling

Ask the participants, "When you become a child of God, what riches do you inherit? What responsibilities do you have?" Encourage them to write their thoughts in their journal.

Closing Prayer

Take turns reading and reflecting upon each of the baptismal promises. End the session with this prayer:

Lord Jesus Christ, give us the grace to fulfill our baptismal promises each day of our lives as we strive to die to self and rise with you. Thank you for this sacrament, for washing away original and personal sin, and for raising us up to a life of grace. Amen.

Looking Ahead

At times in Church history, confirmation immediately followed baptism. Most cradle Catholics today experience a gap between the reception of these two sacraments, but as they are both necessary for full Christian initiation, they are still treated as one in the RCIA process. Lessons C4: *The Sacrament of Confirmation* and C5: *The Sacrament of the Eucharist* cover the remaining two sacraments of initiation.

The Sacrament of Baptism

C4: The Sacrament of Confirmation

Catechism: 1285–1321

Objectives

Participants will…

- identify some of the effects or graces of confirmation: sealing of our Catholic Christian identity and bond with the Church; strength to grow in holiness, to witness for the faith, to fulfill one's vocation, and so on that empower us as witnesses to our faith.

- describe the signs, the laying on of hands and anointing with sacred chrism, that confer the sacrament.

- recall the seven gifts of the Holy Spirit as reflected in Isaiah 11 (*CCC* 1831) and how they help us live as Christ's disciples.

Leader Meditation

Acts 8:14–17

All confirmed Catholics have witnessed the fulfillment of Jesus' promise to send the Holy Spirit. This Spirit comes, as promised, with the power to make us witnesses to the whole world. Your witness—that is, your daily love-filled, Christ-centered living—is your most effective tool in passing on the faith to the people under your guidance.

Related *Catholic Updates*

- "Confirmation: A Deepening of Our Christian Identity" (C9510A)
- "Opening the Gifts of the Holy Spirit" (C9802A)

Leader Preparation

- Read the lesson, this lesson plan, the opening Scripture, and the *Catechism* sections.

- While the whole lesson discusses confirmation, the term is defined in this guide's glossary as well.

- Review the Church's guidelines on sponsors, godparents, and choosing a sacramental or saint's name. The *Journey of Faith* leader guides discuss the former, and the lesson plan for Q15: *The Saints* explains the norms for naming in the context of the RCIA. Instruct catechists and sponsors as needed. If participants inquire about these traditions, encourage them to embrace their current name(s) and to devote themselves to any saint they desire.

Welcome

Greet each person as he or she arrives. Check for supplies and immediate needs. Solicit questions or comments about the previous session and/or share new information and findings. Begin promptly.

Opening Scripture

Acts 8:14–17

Light the candle and read the passage aloud. Explain that the symbolic action described here, the laying on of hands, remains an essential part of the confirmation rite today. It is also used in the sacrament of holy orders to confer the Spirit and a special power and authority. Ask, "What gifts or abilities do I hope to obtain as a full-fledged Catholic?"

> The reception of the sacrament of confirmation is necessary for the completion of baptismal grace. For "by the sacrament of confirmation, [the baptized] are more perfectly bound to the Church and are enriched with a special strength of the Holy Spirit."
>
> CCC 1285

Journey of Faith for Adults, Catechumenate Leader Guide

Journey of Faith

C4 CATECHUMENATE

In Short:

- Through confirmation, the Spirit empowers us as witnesses.
- Laying on of hands and anointing are actions that confer the sacrament.
- The seven gifts of the Holy Spirit help us live as Christ's disciples.

The Sacrament of Confirmation

Many of us lack confidence when it comes to speaking to others about our faith in Jesus Christ.

Jesus promised the apostles he would give them the courage needed to speak of him to others: "But you will receive power when the holy Spirit comes upon you, and you will be my witnesses in Jerusalem, throughout Judea and Samaria, and to the ends of the earth" (Acts 1:8).

Jesus kept his promise. When they received the Holy Spirit, the apostles immediately went out to preach the good news. If they had any reluctance or fear, it was forgotten.

> "When the time for Pentecost was fulfilled, they were all in one place together. And suddenly there came from the sky a noise like a strong driving wind, and it filled the entire house in which they were. Then there appeared to them tongues as of fire, which parted and came to rest on each one of them. And they were all filled with the holy Spirit and began to speak in different tongues, as the Spirit enabled them to proclaim."
>
> *Acts 2:1–4*

Christ fulfills his promise to us as well through the sacrament of confirmation. In confirmation, we receive courage and other gifts of the Holy Spirit we need to be witnesses to Christ in our daily lives.

- How comfortable are you with sharing your faith?

Confirmed for Witness

The word **confirmation** means "strengthening." The *Catechism* says the sacrament of confirmation "both confirms baptism and strengthens baptismal grace" (*CCC* 1289). Believers have the Spirit, our God-breath, from baptism. But the Spirit at confirmation is the breath behind speech, giving us the power to raise our voices in witness.

A witness testifies to what is known from personal experience. Christian witness is a believer's testimony to what they know: Jesus Christ, crucified and risen, is life and hope for all the world. Christians can witness in a variety of ways, from simple, everyday ways such as enthusiastic words or concern for others to dramatic ways such as dying for their faith as a martyr.

ADULTS

CCC 1285–1321

The Sacrament of Confirmation

Read the introductory paragraphs aloud, then ask the participants how they feel when the topic of faith is brought up in social situations. Is it difficult to talk about? Can they openly proclaim their faith around others, or do they (like the apostles huddled in the upper room) prefer to keep their religious formation and/or spirituality to themselves? What courage do they need to live out their faith?

Emphasize that confirmation is a sacrament of initiation; it completes what baptism begins. Discuss the ways that confirmation continues or completes our baptism.

Through the Holy Spirit we receive the courage to live our faith and evangelize to others.

Saint Augustine hints at the difference when he explains that in baptism we are mixed with water so that we might take on the form of bread, the body of Christ. But bread, he points out, needs to be baked in the fire; and this fire is supplied by "the sacrament of the Holy Spirit," who was revealed in tongues of fire.

Confirmed for Witness

Explain that confirmation is a sacrament of Christian witness and maturity. The gifts of the Holy Spirit will empower them to become more fully immersed in the life of the Church.

Define the Holy Spirit as "breath of God" (*ruah*) so that participants can understand the lesson's reference to the Spirit as "our God-breath,…the breath behind speech, giving us the power to raise our voices in witness."

The Sacrament of Confirmation

How Is the Sacrament Celebrated?

Emphasize that the three sacraments of initiation (baptism, confirmation, and the eucharist) lay the foundation for every Catholic Christian life. We are born anew in baptism, are strengthened through confirmation, and receive the food for eternal life in the Eucharist (*CCC* 1212).

Clarify, if necessary, that because Protestant churches lack apostolic succession, the Roman Catholic Church does not consider confirmations celebrated within those denominations as valid. Candidates from these backgrounds will receive a valid confirmation at the Easter Vigil. Individuals from other churches and rites should approach the pastor to determine their needs.

"By the sacrament of Confirmation, [the baptized] are more perfectly bound to the Church and are enriched with a special strength of the Holy Spirit. Hence they are, as true witnesses of Christ, more strictly obliged to spread and defend the faith by word and deed."

CCC 1285

"Do not worry about how you are to speak or what you are to say. You will be given at that moment what you are to say. For it will not be you who speak but the Spirit of your Father speaking through you."

Matthew 10:19–20

Other Confirmation Facts

"The effect of the sacrament of Confirmation is the special outpouring of the Holy Spirit as once granted to the apostles on the day of Pentecost" (*CCC* 1302). The *Catechism* also points out that confirmation:

- "perfects Baptismal grace; it is the sacrament which gives the Holy Spirit in order to root us more deeply in the divine filiation, incorporate us more firmly into Christ, strengthen our bond with the Church, associate us more closely with her mission, and help us bear witness to the Christian faith in words accompanied by deeds" (*CCC* 1316).
- "imprints a spiritual mark or indelible character on the Christian's soul; for this reason one can receive this sacrament only once in one's life" (*CCC* 1317).
- "is necessary for the completion of baptismal grace" (*CCC* 1285).

How Is the Sacrament Celebrated?

Confirmation is usually celebrated during Mass. Adults in the RCIA process are confirmed at the Easter Vigil Mass on Holy Saturday. It's normally the bishop who administers the sacrament, but a priest may do so under circumstances such as at the Easter Vigil Mass.

The sacrament of confirmation is conferred by the *laying on of hands* followed by an *anointing* in the form of a cross with chrism on the forehead. As the candidate for confirmation approaches the bishop (or priest), the sponsor places a hand on the candidate's shoulder as a sign of presenting the candidate on behalf of the Christian community.

The power of the Holy Spirit is invoked with the laying on of hands and praying for the gift of the Spirit. The laying on of hands is a biblical gesture that reflects the significance of human touch. In the Gospels, Jesus healed many people with a touch. When Jesus encountered two blind men, he "touched their eyes. Immediately they received their sight, and followed him" (Matthew 20:34).

Following a prayer for the sevenfold gift of the Spirit, the minister of the sacrament dips his thumb in the holy oil (chrism), makes the sign of the cross on the forehead of the one to be confirmed, and prays: "[Name], be sealed with the gift of the Holy Spirit." Here, *gift* refers to the Holy Spirit. We are sealed with the gift of ("the gift that is") the Holy Spirit. Following this blessing, the bishop (or priest) and the newly confirmed exchange a sign of peace.

"Anointing, in Biblical and other ancient symbolism, is rich in meaning: oil is a sign of abundance and joy; it cleanses (anointing before and after a bath) and limbers (the anointing of athletes and wrestlers); oil is a sign of healing, since it is soothing to bruises and wounds; and it makes radiant with beauty, health, and strength."

CCC 1293

Journey of Faith for Adults, Catechumenate Leader Guide

The Israelites anointed priests, and later kings, as a sign that they were chosen by God. Like these priests and kings, you're chosen by God. And like them, you are being anointed, chosen, for a purpose.

Anointing "signifies and imprints: a spiritual seal" that "marks our total belonging to Christ, our enrollment in his service forever" (CCC 1293, 1296). Those confirmed "share more completely in the mission of Jesus Christ and the fullness of the Holy Spirit...so that their lives may give off 'the aroma of Christ' (2 Corinthians 2:15)" (CCC 1294).

Gifts of the Holy Spirit

The biblical origin of the seven gifts of the Holy Spirit foretells the qualities of the Messiah:

> *"The spirit of the Lord shall rest upon him: a spirit of wisdom and of understanding, A spirit of counsel and of strength, a spirit of knowledge and of fear of the Lord, and his delight shall be the fear of the Lord."*
>
> Isaiah 11:2–3

The word *Messiah—Christos* in Greek—means "anointed." When we're anointed in baptism and confirmation, we "put on Christ" and the qualities of the Messiah become our qualities:

- **Wisdom:** Wisdom moves our vision into the future, giving us perspective and enabling us to see things with God's eyes. The gift of wisdom helps us see our joys and sufferings in the light of God's loving plan for us.

- **Understanding:** The world would be easier to understand if it came with instructions. Fortunately, God's gift of Easter life does come with instructions: the sacred Scriptures. Prayerful reading of the Bible helps us understand God's plan.

- **Right Judgment (Counsel):** This is the gift that helps us to make good choices—God's choices. The gift of right judgment helps us seek God's counsel, God's advice. Right judgments are made in the light of God's great Final Judgment.

- **Courage (Fortitude):** Courage enables us to face danger and overcome fear with confidence. Before performing a cure, Jesus often told his followers to take courage, take heart, be confident. The gift of courage enables us to see where our real strength lies—in God.

- **Knowledge:** The gift of knowledge helps us to know Jesus and to discern which things are important and which aren't. A good way to tell if we're really using the gift of knowledge is to examine whether the things we know lead us to charity in our actions.

- **Reverence (Piety):** Placing us at the foot of Jesus' cross, this gift helps us see our relationship to God: the saved and the Savior. It enables us to act in the light of this reality and to show our gratitude by our piety and devotion.

- **Wonder and Awe in God's Presence (Fear of the Lord):** It takes time and leisure to wonder and be amazed, to see God's beauty around us. We might recall the feeling of looking at something amazing in nature and saying "Wow!" That is this gift in action.

CATECHUMENATE · JOURNEY OF FAITH

C4

Gifts of the Holy Spirit

Review the seven gifts, clarifying any slight variations in wording if necessary. Remind participants that they will receive each of these gifts when they are confirmed.

Go around the room and invite each participant to name one gift, one quality, with which they relate, strongly desire, or already see manifested in a partial way in themselves. Affirm each response and have the participants record them in their journals and to ask God for all these gifts in prayer. Each gift is beneficial and has unique value.

The Sacrament of Confirmation

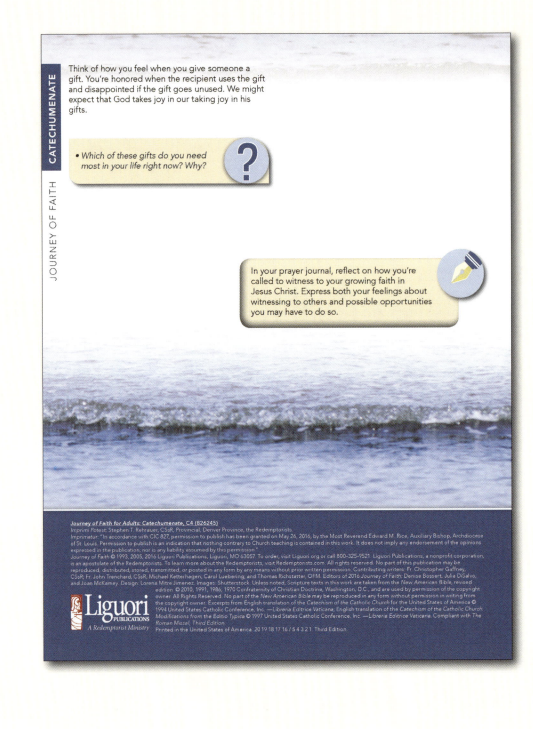

Think of how you feel when you give someone a gift. You're honored when the recipient uses the gift and disappointed if the gift goes unused. We might expect that God takes joy in our taking joy in his gifts.

- Which of these gifts do you need most in your life right now? Why?

In your prayer journal, reflect on how you're called to witness to your growing faith in Jesus Christ. Express both your feelings about witnessing to others and possible opportunities you may have to do so.

Journey of Faith for Adults: Catechumenate, C4 (826245)
Imprimi Potest: Stephen T. Rehrauer, CSsR, Provincial, Denver Province, the Redemptorists.
Imprimatur: "In accordance with CIC 827, permission to publish has been granted on May 26, 2016, by the Most Reverend Edward M. Rice, Auxiliary Bishop, Archdiocese of St. Louis. Permission to publish is an indication that nothing contrary to Church teaching is contained in this work. It does not imply any endorsement of the opinions expressed in the publication, nor is any liability assumed by this permission."
Journey of Faith © 1993, 2005, 2016 Liguori Publications, Liguori, MO 63057. To order, visit Liguori.org or call 800-325-9521. Liguori Publications, a nonprofit corporation, is an apostolate of the Redemptorists. To learn more about the Redemptorists, visit Redemptorists.com. All rights reserved. No part of this publication may be reproduced, distributed, stored, transmitted, or posted in any form by any means without prior written permission. Contributing writers: Fr. Christopher Gaffney, CSsR; Fr. John Trenchard, CSsR; Michael Ketterhagen; Carol Luebering; and Thomas Richstatter, OFM. Editors of 2016 Journey of Faith: Denise Bossert, Julia DiSalvo, and Joan McKamey. Design: Lorena Mitre Jimenez. Images: Shutterstock. Unless noted, Scripture texts in this work are taken from the *New American Bible*, revised edition © 2010, 1991, 1986, 1970 Confraternity of Christian Doctrine, Washington, D.C., and are used by permission of the copyright owner. All Rights Reserved. No part of the *New American Bible* may be reproduced in any form without permission in writing from the copyright owner. Excerpts from English translation of the *Catechism of the Catholic Church* for the United States of America © 1994 United States Catholic Conference, Inc. —Libreria Editrice Vaticana; English translation of the *Catechism of the Catholic Church: Modifications from the Editio Typica* © 1997 United States Catholic Conference, Inc. —Libreria Editrice Vaticana. Compliant with *The Roman Missal, Third Edition*.
Printed in the United States of America. 20 19 18 17 16 / 5 4 3 2 1. Third Edition.

Journey of Faith for Adults, Catechumenate Leader Guide

Journaling

Remind catechumens that as they are still uninitiated, they are not expected to know everything or even permitted to speak with authority. Nevertheless, their willingness to attend Mass and the sessions and to publicly declare their desire for initiation (at the rite of acceptance) is a witness to others, including parishioners whose faith may be faltering.

Encourage candidates to refine their witness and lived example to the fullness of Catholic truth as they grow in understanding. This may confuse or frustrate others, even close friends and relatives, but it may also become a means of evangelization.

Closing Prayer

Prayer to the Holy Spirit (Come, Holy Spirit)

Come, Holy Spirit, fill the hearts of your faithful.
And kindle in them the fire of your love.

Send forth your Spirit and they shall be created.
And you will renew the face of the earth.

Lord, by the light of the Holy Spirit you have taught the hearts of your faithful. In the same Spirit help us to relish what is right and always rejoice in your consolation. We ask this through Christ our Lord. Amen.

Take-home

Encourage each participant to spend some time this week with his or her sponsor and to share more deeply with this companion on the journey of faith.

The Sacrament of Confirmation

C5: The Sacrament of the Eucharist

Catechism: 1322–1419

Objective

Participants will…

- explain the scriptural context of Catholic teachings on the Eucharist, as given through Jesus' words and actions.

- recognize that Catholics affirm that the Eucharist is truly Jesus' body, blood, soul, and divinity.

- realize that Christian disciples model Jesus in being food for the world, giving of themselves, and nourishing the faith of others.

Leader Meditation

John 6:25–51

Belief in the Real Presence of our Lord in the Eucharist sets Catholics apart from many other Christian churches. This passage proclaims the central truth upon which all Catholic teachings are based. Our faith must be like that of the apostles, who through Peter declared, "Master, to whom shall we go? You have the words of eternal life" (John 6:68).

Spend some time before the Blessed Sacrament and ask for the grace to pass on this teaching in a way that is accessible to each participant. Ask yourself, "Is the Eucharist the source and summit of my faith and life? Do I show proper reverence for and in the Mass?"

Related *Catholic Updates*

- "Finding Jesus in the Eucharist: Four Ways He Is Present" (C0507A)

- "Real Presence: Jesus' Gift to the Church" (C0109A)

- "From Worship to World: Sent Forth as the Body of Christ" (C1409A)

Leader Preparation

- Read the lesson, this lesson plan, the opening Scripture, and the *Catechism* sections.

- Be familiar with the vocabulary word term transubstantiation. It is explained in the lesson and defined in this guide's glossary. Equip yourself to answer basic questions about this dogma, but don't hesitate to refer difficult or complex matters to a priest.

- Arrange your meeting space so the seating forms a circle around a small prayer table, image of Jesus, or other sacramentals. Ask to borrow a sacred vessel or two from the sacristy: a ciborium, chalice, paten, pyx, or monstrance.

- Invite an extraordinary minister of holy Communion or member of a liturgical or eucharistic ministry to speak to the participants about his or her role, responsibilities, and experiences with distributing Communion, visiting the sick and homebound, preparing for or cleaning up after Mass, and other activities.

- Invite your pastor to incorporate a short period of adoration or a special Benediction into this session or during this week. It would be particularly moving if the parish joined in this experience, so take the time to invite the friends and family of RCIA members and to share the details with parishioners and local ministries.

Welcome

Greet each person as he or she arrives. When all are gathered, remind them that we are one in Christ, members of his body—even catechumens. Explain the format or schedule of the session, if needed. Begin promptly.

Opening Scripture

John 6:25–51

Light the candle and proclaim the passage. Explain that this Scripture, along with similar passages, accounts of the Last Supper, and early-Church writings and traditions, form the basis of the Catholic Church's understanding of the Eucharist. Invite participants to respond and share their reactions.

The mode of Christ's presence under the Eucharistic species is unique. It raises the Eucharist above all the sacraments as "the perfection of the spiritual life and the end to which all the sacraments tend."
CCC 1374

Journey of Faith

CATECHUMENATE — C5

In Short:
- Catholic teaching on the Eucharist is based on Jesus' words and actions.
- Catholics believe in the Real Presence of Jesus in the Eucharist.
- Christians are called to imitate Christ by being bread for others.

The Sacrament of the Eucharist

Some Scripture scholars believe that what most scandalized and infuriated the Jewish leaders about Jesus was that he ate meals with outcasts. He welcomed the despised tax collectors and sinners into table fellowship with him.

Centuries of tradition had given all formal meals among devout Jews a religious significance. Meals became symbols of the past when God had rescued their Hebrew ancestors from slavery and formed a covenant with them. Meals also symbolized the future when the faithful would share in a heavenly banquet.

Seeing Jesus sharing meals with outcasts, the chief priests and elders objected. They asked, *How could he not know who these people are? Doesn't he realize that by eating with them, he's offending God?*

Jesus was well aware of those he was eating with. The official list of "sinners" included not only thieves, murderers, adulterers, extortionists, and prostitutes, but another group even further down the list—those Jews who worked for Gentiles (like swineherds and tax collectors). By eating with them, Jesus was, in essence, welcoming these outcasts back into the community.

The conviction that God was on their side was what upheld the Israelites in the midst of many afflictions. Then Jesus came along, claiming they were mistaken about God's attitude toward those same people they refused to tolerate. Jesus constantly demonstrated how wrong they were by living out what he taught. It was clear that Jesus ate with these outcasts not just for private motives but in the name of the kingdom of God!

No wonder they were angry enough to have him executed.

> "Some scribes who were Pharisees saw that he was eating with sinners and tax collectors and said to his disciples, 'Why does he eat with tax collectors and sinners?' Jesus heard this and said to them [that], 'Those who are well do not need a physician, but the sick do. I did not come to call the righteous but sinners.'"
>
> *Mark 2:16–17*

- What significance do you connect with sharing a meal?
- What kinds of outcasts would you invite to share a meal with you?

ADULTS

CCC 1322–1419

The Sacrament of the Eucharist

Discuss the importance of sharing meals together, both at the time of Jesus and today. Ask participants, "What mealtime or food-related traditions do you keep?"

Ask participants, "What does Jesus' desire to break bread with everyone—even outcasts—tell us about him? How do his actions model how we should treat the outcasts in our families, neighborhoods, and workplaces?"

Suggested responses include: he wants everyone to feel welcome, we are all part of Jesus' family—even sinners; Jesus wants a personal relationship with everyone.

The Sacrament of the Eucharist

The Eucharist as Meal

Explain that the Eucharist is a commemoration and a re-presentation (*not* a repetition or reenactment) of Christ's passion and death. Consider reading these words of St. Alphonsus Liguori:

"How pleasing it is to Jesus Christ that we remember his Passion, since he has instituted the sacrament of the altar, that we may preserve a continual remembrance of the immense love which he has shown us…."

The Eucharist as Sacrifice

Describe how the Eucharist is both a meal and a sacrifice.

Suggested responses include: Just as table fellowship was important to Jesus' culture, it is also important to us as Catholics. By sharing the Eucharist as a meal with our brothers and sisters in Christ, we are showing our camaraderie with each other. Unlike the Jewish households of Jesus' time who offered sacrifices to God such as animals or fruits of their harvest, Catholics believe Jesus' death on the cross was the ultimate sacrifice. Every Mass, Jesus is re-presented as that sacrifice. We celebrate the "memorial of his sacrifice" and "offer to the Father what he has himself given us: the gifts of creation" (CCC 1357).

The Eucharist as Meal

The meals Jesus shared with sinners and outcasts add to the significance of his farewell meal with his apostles.

During this Last Supper, Jesus spelled out how the Father's forgiveness and the New Covenant, the promise of eternal life in Christ, would come about. He spelled it out by *word*, saying, "This is my body…. This is my blood of the covenant" (Mark 14:22, 24). He spelled it out in *action* through the sharing of bread and wine.

He also spoke of the price to be paid for the New Covenant to take place. This meal was a powerful message for the apostles. If they truly heeded his words and actions, if they lived up to what this meal required of them, they, like Jesus, should be ready, if necessary, to lay down their lives for others—as Jesus would do.

> *"While they were eating, Jesus took bread, said the blessing, broke it, and giving it to his disciples said, 'Take and eat; this is my body.' Then he took a cup, gave thanks, and gave it to them, saying, 'Drink from it, all of you, for this is my blood of the covenant, which will be shed on behalf of many for the forgiveness of sins.'"*
>
> Matthew 26:26–28

The Eucharist as Sacrifice

The meaning of sacrifice to people in biblical times is foreign to our culture and experience. A Jewish family coming to the Temple to offer sacrifice didn't bring gold but something connected with life, such as a living animal or fruits of the harvest. The sacrifice occurred when the priest put the fruits or blood on the altar and the people made an internal offering of *themselves*. The most important part of the sacrifice was what happened in people's minds and hearts—the offering of their lives to God.

Jesus' death on the cross was the greatest of all sacrifices. Jesus made an offering of himself. The Mass is the free sacrificial offering of Jesus.

But the Mass is not trying to replicate either the ancient sacrifices of the Temple ritual or the bloody event of Jesus' death. The ritual gestures performed by the priest at Mass aren't a stylized reenactment of the slaying of Jesus. The Lord could die only once; he will never die again. Rather, it's in celebrating this family meal, which we call the Mass, that we unite ourselves with Jesus' act of will and offer ourselves to God, mirroring the self-dedication Jesus had when he died on the cross.

> *"This sacrifice of Christ is unique; it completes and surpasses all other sacrifices. First, it is a gift from God the Father himself, for the Father handed his Son over to sinners in order to reconcile us with himself. At the same time it is the offering of the Son of God made man, who in freedom and love offered his life to his Father through the Holy Spirit in reparation for our disobedience."*
>
> CCC 614

- What does Christ's sacrifice for our sins mean to you personally?

Journey of Faith for Adults, Catechumenate Leader Guide

The Real Presence of Christ

Catholics believe that when Jesus said, "This is my body...This is my blood," he meant exactly what he said. For Jews, body meant the person, and blood was the source of the person's life. So Jesus was saying over the bread and cup, "This is myself," and we believe the consecrated bread and wine truly become the very person of Jesus.

The New Testament bears witness to the reality of Christ's presence in the Eucharist. Chapter 6 of John's Gospel is devoted to Jesus as the "Bread of Life":

- Jesus multiplies loaves and fish, a miracle that foreshadows his ability to "multiply his presence" in the Eucharist (see John 6:1–15).
- When he walks on water, he shows his divine power over nature, a power capable of changing bread into his Body (see John 6:16–21).
- Jesus teaches what is called his "Bread of Life Discourse" (see John 6:22–59).

"Jesus himself tells us: 'I am the living bread that came down from heaven; whoever eats this bread will live forever; and the bread that I will give is my flesh for the life of the world. Whoever eats my flesh and drinks my blood has eternal life, and I will raise him on the last day.'"

John 6:51, 54

Many disciples found these words about eating Jesus' flesh and drinking his blood intolerable and left him. But Jesus didn't say, "Wait, I meant that the bread *only represents* my body." Instead, he asked the Twelve, "'Do you also want to leave?' Simon Peter answered him, 'Master, to whom shall we go? You have the words of eternal life'" (John 6:67–68).

Since the twelfth century, the Church has used the word **transubstantiation** to describe the change from the *substance* of bread and wine to the *substance* of the flesh and blood of Christ.

The *appearances*—the outer aspects like taste, color, and weight—remain just as they were before the consecration, but the deep realities have been changed into the Body and Blood of the living Christ.

When we receive holy Communion, *we receive the whole person of Christ*, as he is at the present moment—risen Lord, with his glorified body and soul, and his full divinity.

"Dying for us did not satisfy you. You had to give us this sacrament as a companion, as food, as a pledge of heaven. You had to become a tiny baby, a poor laborer, a beaten criminal, even a morsel of bread. Only a God who loves us deeply could conceive such ideas!"

St. Alphonsus Liguori

- How does Jesus in the Eucharist call to you? How do you feel about sharing in the Eucharist?

The Real Presence of Christ

Clarify the doctrine of real presence for candidates coming from faith traditions that view Communion as only a symbolic action.

Compare and contrast outward appearance with inner reality. While one often affects the other, they may not be one and the same.

Emphasize that the Eucharist is mystery. The change—transubstantiation—is a miracle. Christ is truly with us until the end of time.

Have participants read CCC 1377, "The Eucharistic presence of Christ begins at the moment of the consecration and endures as long as the Eucharistic species subsists."

The Sacrament of the Eucharist

Living the Eucharist

Give practical examples of how we become the body of Christ through active participation in the Mass, even without receiving the Eucharist. Invite sponsors and team members to describe what it is to be an active receiver of Christ's divine body and blood and how our participation in this feast contributes to our own and the whole community's spiritual transformation. Remind participants how to make a spiritual communion.

Introduce and listen to the member of the clergy, extraordinary minister, or similar representative. Encourage the presenter to conclude with some time for questions and comments.

Transition to the adoration chapel, benediction, or spend ten minutes privately contemplating the mystery of the Eucharist before the Blessed Sacrament, tabernacle, or sacred vessel(s) in the room (see "Leader Preparation"). Invite participants to repeat this devotion on their own regularly.

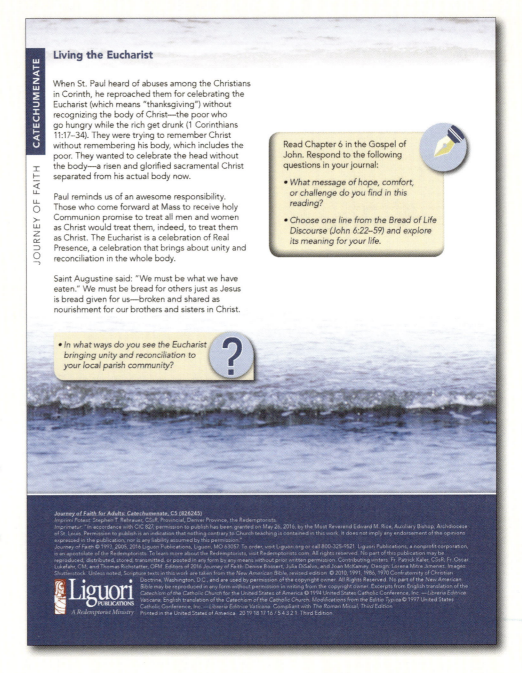

Living the Eucharist

When St. Paul heard of abuses among the Christians in Corinth, he reproached them for celebrating the Eucharist (which means "thanksgiving") without recognizing the body of Christ—the poor who go hungry while the rich get drunk (1 Corinthians 11:17–34). They were trying to remember Christ without remembering his body, which includes the poor. They wanted to celebrate the head without the body—a risen and glorified sacramental Christ separated from his actual body now.

Paul reminds us of an awesome responsibility. Those who come forward at Mass to receive holy Communion promise to treat all men and women as Christ would treat them, indeed, to treat them as Christ. The Eucharist is a celebration of Real Presence, a celebration that brings about unity and reconciliation in the whole body.

Saint Augustine said: "We must be what we have eaten." We must be bread for others just as Jesus is bread given for us—broken and shared as nourishment for our brothers and sisters in Christ.

- In what ways do you see the Eucharist bringing unity and reconciliation to your local parish community?

Read Chapter 6 in the Gospel of John. Respond to the following questions in your journal:

- What message of hope, comfort, or challenge do you find in this reading?
- Choose one line from the Bread of Life Discourse (John 6:22–59) and explore its meaning for your life.

Journey of Faith for Adults: Catechumenate, C5 (826245)

Journaling

Encourage participants to record their thoughts and experiences in their journals. The closing prayer will assist them in responding to the lesson's prompts.

Closing Prayer

Continue the reading of John 6, explaining beforehand that many of Jesus' disciples were confused and discouraged by his words. Some even chose to leave and lost their faith. Proclaim verses 60–69, which end with Peter saying, "We have come to believe and are convinced that you are the Holy One of God." Remind the participants to dwell on the power and love of God rather than the intellectual and spiritual challenges of discipleship. Then recite the prayer below:

Lord, help us to take you at your word, to trust when we feel some of the confusion your first disciples felt, and to persevere in the faith that we, too, may come to know the treasure you have given us in your own body and blood, broken and spilled for our sins, becoming for us the food of everlasting life. Amen.

Looking Ahead

Explain that because we receive God himself in the Eucharist, our most sacred gift, we must receive it in a state of grace. The Church helps us to achieve that through the topic of lesson C6: *The Sacrament of Penance and Reconciliation*. Penance, also known as *confession*, also helps us in our pursuit of holiness and prepares us for judgment and eternal life in heaven.

The Sacrament of the Eucharist

C6: The Sacrament of Penance and Reconciliation

Catechism: 1422–98, 1846–76

Objectives

Participants will…

- realize that while sin may be secret, it is never private.
- recognize that Jesus gave his disciples, the Church, the authority to forgive sins in his name.
- identify the major steps in the sacrament (rite) of penance.
- be able to differentiate between mortal and venial sin.

Leader Meditation

Luke 15:11–32

Read the parable of the Prodigal Son, putting yourself in the father's place—feel his feelings; respond as he reacts. Then do the same with the older son, and finally with the younger son. How many times have you been in similar positions, felt similar feelings, responded in similar ways? When have you yearned for forgiveness? When have you been deeply hurt or disappointed by someone you love? When have you longed to be soothed by the comfort and peace of mercy and reconciliation?

Related *Catholic Updates*

- "The Sacrament of Reconciliation: Celebrating the Mercy of God" (C0906A)
- "Ten Tips for Better Confessions" (C9008A)
- "Learning to Forgive: Steps to Reconciliation" (C1503A)

Leader Preparation

- Read the lesson, this lesson plan, the opening Scripture, and the *Catechism* sections.
- Be familiar with the following vocabulary terms: sin, venial sin, mortal sin, examination of conscience, penance, act of contrition, absolution. Definitions are provided in this guide's glossary.
- Find an examination of conscience to bring as an example. Be prepared to give examples to some of the questions.
- Make the reconciliation chapel or confessional available for display if participants didn't visit this space during their church tour (lesson Q11). If this isn't possible, gather images of such spaces to illustrate their diversity and reduce any anxiety or preconceived notions of the sacrament.

Welcome

Greet each person as they arrive with "Peace be with you," or "The Lord be with you." Check for supplies and immediate needs. Solicit questions or comments about the previous session and/or share new information and findings. Begin promptly.

Opening Scripture

Luke 15:11–32

Light the candle and read the parable of the Prodigal Son aloud. Have the participants meditate on the feelings experienced by the three central figures in the story. Ask them, "To whom do you relate the most? The least?" Encourage them to imagine the love this father felt for his lost son. Remind them that this is only a fraction of the love God has for each of us.

> Those who approach the sacrament of penance obtain pardon from God's mercy for the offense committed against [God], and are, at the same time, reconciled with the Church.
>
> *CCC 1422*

Journey of Faith for Adults, Catechumenate Leader Guide

Journey of Faith

C6 CATECHUMENATE

In Short:
- No sin is hidden from God, and all sins affect the community.
- Jesus forgave sins and gave his apostles the authority to forgive.
- Penance leads us from sorrow for sin to reconciliation with God and Church.

The Sacrament of Penance and Reconciliation

We often wish for chances to receive forgiveness, to redeem past hurts. Recall something you did recently that you regret. Shouting at a driver who cut you off in traffic. Promoting yourself in a way that discounts the efforts of others. *How would you feel about asking for forgiveness?*

Or maybe you were the one who was hurt. Maybe you'd like to offer forgiveness.

Feeling the need to seek and extend forgiveness is common among people of good will. When thoughts, words, or actions have been intentionally unloving, relationships—between people and with God—are affected. Reconciliation is needed.

- How difficult is it for you to ask for forgiveness? To offer forgiveness?

Sin Is a Refusal to Love

Sin isn't merely breaking the rules. Sin is understood in relation to love. God loves us so much, yet we often fail to return that love. **Sin is the failure to respond to the love God has shown us in Christ Jesus.**

Sin is first a matter of a selfish heart—a refusal to care—before it shows itself in actions. Because loving God and loving our neighbor are tied together, sin will always be expressed in and through our relationships. Sin can take the form of words, actions, thoughts, attitudes, and failure to speak or act with love.

In one option of the penitential act at Mass, we confess to sinning "in my thoughts and in my words, in what I have done and in what I have failed to do."

The Effects of Sin

In the creation story found in the Old Testament Book of Genesis, Adam and Eve experienced harmony with self, God, each other, and creation until the serpent entered the Garden and they committed sin. In Genesis 3 (see verses below), we see the effects of disobeying God.

Alienation From Self
After Adam and Eve sinned, their eyes "were opened, and they knew that they were naked; so they sewed fig leaves together and made loincloths" (7). Shame and uneasiness replaced openness and confidence.

ADULTS

CCC 1422–98, 1846–76

The Sacrament of Penance and Reconciliation

Read the lesson's opening section aloud and then invite the participants to recall and share experiences of sin and forgiveness from their own lives.

Sin Is a Refusal to Love

Discuss the description of sin found in this section. Emphasize the beauty of the gifts of forgiveness and healing. Acknowledge that confessing one's sins to another person can be frightening to those who have never received—or who rarely approach—the sacrament.

The Sacrament of Penance and Reconciliation

How Did Jesus Minister to Sinners?

Share these responses with participants as needed:

- Mark 2:1–12, the healing of a paralytic, "When Jesus saw their faith, he said to the paralytic, 'Child, your sins are forgiven….I say to you, rise, pick up your mat, and go home.'"
  Jesus coupled the man's spiritual healing with physical healing and offered words of comfort and mission.

- Luke 7:36–50 "[Jesus] turned to the woman and said to Simon, 'Do you see this woman? …I tell you, her many sins have been forgiven; hence, she has shown great love…' He said to her, 'Your sins are forgiven….Your faith has saved you; go in peace.'"
  Jesus justifies her gesture, acknowledges her faith and love, and forgives her sins.

- Luke 19:1–10, Zacchaeus the tax collector, "Jesus looked up and said to him, 'Zacchaeus, come down quickly, for today I must stay at your house…. Today salvation has come to this house because this man too is a descendant of Abraham.'"
  Jesus invites Zacchaeus into fellowship, accepts his acts of justice (penance), and declares salvation to his house.

- John 8:1–11, a woman caught in adultery, "Jesus bent down and began to write on the ground with his finger. But when they continued asking him, he straightened up and said to them, 'Let the one among you who is without sin be the first to throw a stone at her.' ….Then Jesus [said], 'Woman, where are they? Has no one condemned you?...Neither do I condemn you. Go, [and] from now on do not sin any more.'"

Jesus judges her with mercy and exhorts her not to sin any more. By exposing the sinfulness of others, he employs the Golden Rule.

CATECHUMENATE / JOURNEY OF FAITH

When we sin, the nakedness of trust is replaced by a cloak of defensiveness. No matter how attractive and pleasurable sin may seem, it has a diminishing and disintegrating effect on our inner selves.

Alienation From God
They "hid themselves from the Lord God among the trees of the garden" (8). Fear and distance replaced the trust and intimacy they previously had with God. Uncomfortable in God's presence, they hid.

When we sin, we distance ourselves from God, thinking we're unworthy of God's love.

Alienation From Others
"The woman whom you put here with me—she gave me fruit from the tree, so I ate it" (12). Adam blamed Eve for leading him into disobedience just as Eve blamed the serpent. As a result, Adam and Eve became alienated from each other. Our self-centeredness alienates us from others. Sin introduces division.

How Did Jesus Minister to Sinners?

Jesus came to reconcile and save us. He communicated healing and mercy in a human way. He also gave his apostles the power to forgive sins: "he breathed on them and said to them, 'Receive the holy Spirit. Whose sins you forgive are forgiven them, and whose sins you retain are retained'" (John 20:22–23). The Church continues Jesus' ministry of reconciliation today in the sacrament of penance and reconciliation.

Forgiving sins was central to Jesus' ministry. Read the following Gospel passages and consider how Jesus ministered to the sinner in each:

Mark 2:1–12   Luke 7:36–50

Luke 19:1–10   John 8:1–11

- How do you feel about God forgiving your sins?

Types of Sin

Every sin falls into one of two categories:

- **Venial sin** occurs when we fail to show care for others. We may speak sharply, revel in gossip, or exercise inappropriate power over another. Venial sins don't radically turn us away from God, but the habit of unloving acts can corrode our relationship to God. We must take venial sins seriously because they can weigh us down with bad habits.

- **Mortal sin** seriously breaks the relationship with God, neighbor, world, and self. Three conditions are needed for a sin to be considered mortal (see *CCC* 1857):
  - The act is wrong (grave matter).
  - The person knows it's wrong (full knowledge).
  - The person chooses to do it anyway (deliberate consent).

The Steps of the Rite

The sacrament of penance and reconciliation can be celebrated individually or in a communal service. Both rites include individual confession and absolution.

Contrition
We prepare for the sacrament through an **examination of conscience**, reflecting on our lives and the choices we've made. We may use the Ten Commandments and teachings of Jesus to guide our examination. We reflect on how generous—or selfish—our responses to God and others have been.

To be forgiven, we must show contrition, sorrow for our sins, and be resolved to follow Jesus' command to the woman caught in adultery, "from now on do not sin any more" (John 8:11).

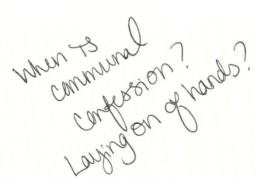

[handwritten note: When is communal confession? Laying on of hands?]

Types of Sin

Emphasize that distinguishing between mortal and venial sin is more than determining the seriousness of a sin or taking account of its negative effects. One may objectively commit a *grave* or *serious* offense, but because of incomplete knowledge or consent not be guilty of mortal sin. Rather than becoming complacent or scrupulous, encourage participants to avoid temptation and sin in practical ways and to form their consciences according to Church teaching.

Journey of Faith for Adults, Catechumenate Leader Guide

Confessing Sins, Accepting a Penance

We admit our sinfulness and confess our sins. Perhaps a Scripture passage made us aware of an area in which we haven't loved enough. "Father, I'm like the older son in the gospel you read, and I'm not ready to forgive others." Or, "I'm often impatient with my family." Or, "I have sinned and I desire absolution."

The priest will assign a **penance**. The act of penance—often a prayer, Scripture reading, or action—helps heal us of the sin and, in some way, makes up for the damage our sin caused.

Why Confess to a Priest?

We don't live in our minds alone; we need to express—with words, signs, and gestures—what's in our minds and hearts. We need to see, hear, and feel forgiveness—not just think about it.

While sin may be secret, it's never private. The Church has always believed that every sin affects the entire community. Since our sins wound and diminish the community, reconciliation must include the community, not just God. In the sacrament, the priest represents Christ (the head) and the Church (the members).

As Jesus' stand-in, the priest isn't learning anything new; God sees all our actions. And like God, he wants only to offer mercy. He is also bound by the seal of the confessional: "He can make no use of knowledge that confession gives him about penitents' lives" (*CCC* 1467). So in this sense only, all our sins remain private.

Act of Contrition, Absolution

We express sorrow for our sins in an **act of contrition**. We may express sorrow in our own words, the priest may lead us in prayer, or we may use a memorized prayer like this one:

> My God, I am sorry for my sins with all my heart. In choosing to do wrong and failing to do good, I have sinned against you whom I should love above all things. I firmly intend, with your help, to do penance, to sin no more, and to avoid whatever leads me to sin. Our Savior Jesus Christ suffered and died for us. In his name, my God, have mercy. Amen.

The priest extends his right hand over us and makes the prayer of **absolution**. Hearing God's forgiveness with our ears meets a basic human need. This prayer completes, seals, our change of heart. It signifies God's forgiveness of us and our reconciliation with the Church:

> "...May God give you pardon and peace, and I absolve you from your sins in the name of the Father, and of the Son, and of the Holy Spirit."
>
> *Rite of Penance*, 46

When we leave the reconciliation chapel, we've been forgiven of the sins we confessed and the sins we unintentionally omitted. We perform our penance and make a new beginning.

James 5:16, 19-20

The Steps of the Rite

Explain that the Church refers to this sacrament in several ways: the *sacrament of penance*, the *sacrament of confession*, the *sacrament of forgiveness*, and the *sacrament of reconciliation* (*CCC* 1423–24).

Review the steps of the rite and accompanying dispositions. Remind them that examinations, penances, and acts of contrition can vary but will always occur. Invite sponsors and team members to share their general (not specific) experiences.

Why Confess to a Priest? Must He Know?

Discuss why penance, like all the sacraments, belongs to the faith community and not just to the individual and God. For a moving account of the sacrament's purpose and power, read or direct participants to Pope Francis' general audience of February 19, 2014.

Remind participants, especially candidates who will receive their first penance before the Easter Vigil, that priests are "bound under very severe penalties [excommunication] to keep absolute secrecy regarding the sins that his penitents have confessed..." (*CCC* 1467, see Canon 1388). Assure them that no priest will view or treat anyone differently because of a sin; they are sinners, too. Many priests have said that they have heard every sin in the book and/or have no desire to remember them—once absolved, they are gone forever.

The Sacrament of Penance and Reconciliation

How Often Should I Celebrate This Sacrament?

Mention that baptized candidates are eligible to receive this sacrament and should before the Easter Vigil. Let them know if your parish will schedule a special day or time for RCIA or Lenten confessions.

Remind catechumens that their baptisms will wash them clean of all sin. They will not receive the sacrament of penance until it is needed, after initiation.

How Often Should I Celebrate This Sacrament?

We're encouraged to do so often enough that when we really need the sacrament, it doesn't feel like an alien or strange experience. It should feel like coming home. Many people find more frequent, even monthly, celebration of this sacrament to be helpful. Catholics are obligated to confess serious sins at least once a year. Mortal sins must be named explicitly, number and type, in the sacrament of penance and reconciliation (Canon 988, CCC 1456).

Advent and Lent are traditional times when the Church beckons her children to know and celebrate God's mercy in this sacrament. Most parishes provide communal penance services or schedule extra times for reception of the sacrament. Parishes also offer regular times throughout the year, such as Saturday afternoons, and anyone can request an appointment with a priest.

Ambassadors of Reconciliation

We're called to be God's instruments in removing barriers that keep individuals and groups from communicating with and caring for one another. Participation in this sacrament implies that as God freely forgives our transgressions, we also are willing to freely give and receive forgiveness. As we pray in the Our Father: "Forgive us our trespasses as we forgive those who trespass against us."

The sacrament of penance is a sacrament of both human and divine dimensions. All of us sin and all of us stand in need of forgiveness. Ours is a God who heals, a physician who binds up our wounded hearts, a loving parent who forgives and embraces the child who has wandered off. In this sacrament, God offers the same mercy and care to us.

- Name a way you can answer the call to forgive.

Begin to document a regular examination of conscience in your journal. Record the highs and lows of your ongoing journey toward right living and right relationship with God, others, and yourself.

- What are the stumbling blocks that lead me to sin?
- What sins weigh heavy on my heart?

Journey of Faith for Adults, Catechumenate Leader Guide

Journaling

Explain to participants that their examinations should be short and simple and never result in scrupulosity. The goal is to evaluate their role in their relationship with Christ, not to create a laundry list of sins.

Mention, if there's time and it helps, that some Catholics practice a general *examen*. This daily method was proposed by St. Ignatius Loyola in his *Spiritual Exercises*:

1. "Give thanks to God, our Lord, for the benefits received."

2. "Ask grace to know our sins and cast them out."

3. "Ask account of our soul… first as to thoughts, and then as to words, and then as to acts…."

4. "Ask pardon of God, our Lord, for the faults."

5. "Purpose amendment with his grace."

Closing Prayer

Have participants privately ask God for the grace to change or improve one area of their lives. Give some generic examples, for instance, "Lord, give me the grace to be aware of how others feel" or "Lord, soften my tongue, because I often hurt others with my harsh words." After a moment of silence, say, "For all these intentions, we pray to the Lord." The group responds, "Lord, hear our prayer."

Take-home

Invite participants to think of a personal relationship that was (or is) affected by sin and to respond to these questions in their journal:

• What words or actions created injury or disunity? What underlying feelings or beliefs were conveyed? What could have been done differently?

• Have I offered forgiveness to or achieved reconciliation with this person? How did that (or could that) come about? Who made the first move?

• Have I lost this or another relationship because forgiveness was lacking? What challenges or circumstances contributed to this? Who else is affected by this reality? How might God's mercy still enter into the situation and hearts of each person involved?

As they reflect on their desire for God's healing, encourage them to silently dwell on his everlasting presence and love.

The Sacrament of Penance and Reconciliation

C7: The Sacrament of the Anointing of the Sick

Catechism: 1499–1532

Objectives

Participants will…

- identify Jesus' healing ministry as described in Scripture as the basis for this sacrament.
- identify the major themes, steps, and effects of the sacrament.
- recognize that anointing of the sick is not directed exclusively at physical healing or reserved for the end of life, and that its benefits are spiritual and available to anyone in need of strength or healing.

Leader Meditation

James 5:13–16

The early Church saw a great connection between the healing of the body and the healing of the soul. In this lesson, the participants will be asked to distinguish between physical curing and spiritual healing. Reflect on this sacrament's emphasis on restored spiritual and emotional health. Ask yourself, "What kinds of suffering have I witnessed or experienced? What role have faith and prayer played in my perception and response to suffering and pain?"

Related *Catholic Update*

- "Anointing of the Sick: A Parish Sacrament" (C9601A)

Leader Preparation

- Read the lesson, this lesson plan, the opening Scripture, and the *Catechism* sections.
- While the whole lesson discusses the tradition and sacrament of anointing of the sick, the term is defined in this guide's glossary as well.
- Borrow a cruet or image of holy (blessed) oil to display or show participants, unless they are already familiar with the sacramental from their church tour or an earlier lesson.

Welcome

Greet each person as he or she arrives. Check for supplies and immediate needs. Solicit questions or comments about the previous session and/or share new information and findings. Begin promptly.

Opening Scripture

James 5:13–16

Light the candle and read the passage aloud. Explain that like sacred chrism, the oil used for anointing the sick is blessed by the bishop and is an essential symbol of this sacrament. As the reading reveals, anointing has its roots in the early Church. Ask the participants, "What other religious and medicinal practices do you commonly associate with the sick, suffering, and elderly?"

> By the sacred anointing of the sick and the prayer of the priests the whole Church commends those who are ill to the suffering and glorified Lord, that he may raise them up and save them.
>
> CCC 1499

Journey of Faith for Adults, Catechumenate Leader Guide

C7 CATECHUMENATE / ADULTS

In Short:
- Jesus' healing ministry is the basis for this sacrament.
- The entire human being—body and soul—is touched by God's salvation.
- This sacrament includes the laying on of hands and anointing.

The Sacrament of the Anointing of the Sick

Jesus was concerned about people's physical as well as spiritual health. In fact, the word *salvation* is derived from the Latin *salus*, which means "health." In announcing the good news of salvation, Jesus was declaring that God cares for us completely—body, soul, and spirit.

Jesus healed people's spiritual lives by assuring them that God forgives their sins and gives them the power to love and care for others. Jesus also healed people's ailments as a sign of God's power and as an example of caring for the entire person.

By healing people's bodies as well as their souls, Jesus showed that the entire human being is touched by God's salvation.

- *When has your physical health been affected by your mental health or vice versa?*

Throughout the Gospels, we read of Jesus' concern for the sick. Read the following healing accounts from the Gospels of Matthew and Luke, then answer the questions below.

Matthew 8:5–13   Matthew 15:21–28
Luke 5:12–16   Luke 5:17–26

- *What types of ailments did Jesus heal?*
- *What was required in order for Jesus to heal a person?*
- *How were other people involved in these healing stories?*

What Healing Ministry Did Jesus Leave the Church?

Healing was also essential to the mission of the apostles: "[Jesus] summoned the Twelve and began to send them out two by two....They anointed with oil many who were sick and cured them" (Mark 6:7, 13).

After Jesus ascended into heaven, the Church continued to be a sacrament of healing. In the Letter of James, we read: "Is anyone among you sick? He should summon the presbyters of the church, and they should pray over him and anoint [him] with oil in the name of the Lord, and the prayer of faith will save the sick person, and the Lord will raise him up. If he has committed any sins, he will be forgiven" (James 5:14–15).

CCC 1499–1532

The Sacrament of Anointing of the Sick

Discuss the distinction between curing a person's disease or illness and healing a person's body, mind, and spirit. Emphasize the importance of grasping this distinction, especially in relation to this sacrament. Ask the participants to give examples of healing (with or without curing) from their own experiences.

Discuss ways in which physical and spiritual well-being are closely connected. Ask, "How does our appearance and behavior change when we are under stress? How do our bodies react when we endure prolonged periods of stress, strain, or intense emotion?"

Share these responses with participants as needed:

- Matthew 8:5–13, the healing of a centurion's servant, "A centurion approached [Jesus] and appealed to him, saying, 'Lord, my servant is lying at home paralyzed, suffering dreadfully.' He said to him, 'I will come and cure him.'"
  Jesus cured paralysis; only faith and a sincere, humble request were needed. The centurion (master) sought out Jesus in the servant's stead.

- Matthew 15:21–28, the Canaanite woman's faith, "A Canaanite woman of that district came and called out, 'Have pity on me, Lord, Son of David! My daughter is tormented by a demon. … Please, Lord, for even the dogs eat the scraps that fall from the table of their masters.' Then Jesus said to her in reply, 'O woman, great is your faith!'"
  Jesus exorcised demons; the mother's faith and persistence were needed. The mother begged for her daughter's healing, and the disciples rebuked her.

- Luke 5:12–16, the cleansing of a leper, "Jesus stretched out his hand, touched him, and said, 'I do will it. Be made clean.' And the leprosy left him immediately. Then he ordered him not to tell anyone, but 'Go, show yourself to the priest and offer for your cleansing what Moses prescribed.'"
  Jesus cured leprosy; the laying on of hands, priest's review, and a religious offering were needed. The priest's role was prescribed, and the crowds reacted.

- Luke 5:17–26, the healing of a paralytic, "[Jesus] said to them in reply, '…Which is easier, to say, "Your sins are forgiven," or to say, "Rise and walk?" But that you may know that the Son of Man has authority on earth to forgive sins'—he said to the man who was paralyzed, 'I say to you, rise, pick up your stretcher, and go home.'"
  Jesus cured paralysis; an act of faith was needed. The men who carried and lowered him in played an essential role, and the scribes and Pharisees prompted Jesus' revealing his authority to forgive and heal (divinity).

The Sacrament of Anointing of the Sick

Sickness Involves More Than Bodily Illness

List different forms of illnesses as a group.

Responses may include physical sickness, disease, chronic symptoms, addiction, mental illness, abuse, trauma, family dysfunction, and other social impairments.

Discuss the healing processes involved in several of these forms. Individuals may offer specific examples at their discretion.

Responses may include various treatments and/or procedures, therapies and/or rehabilitation programs, recovery from addiction, psychological counseling, and more.

The sacrament of the **anointing of the sick** is based on Jesus' concern for the sick, his commissioning the apostles to heal the sick, and the healing ministry of the early Church.

Faith in God's Care

To fully celebrate the sacrament of the anointing of the sick, it helps to recognize the following points:

Anointing Is a Community Celebration
The *Catechism* states that when the sick are anointed, they should be "assisted by their pastor and the whole ecclesial community, which is invited to surround the sick in a special way through their prayers and fraternal attention" (*CCC* 1516) and "Like all the sacraments the Anointing of the Sick is a liturgical and communal celebration….It is very fitting to celebrate it within the Eucharist" (*CCC* 1517).

A person doesn't have to wait to celebrate the sacrament until an illness is so grave that he or she is in the hospital. This sacrament, like all the sacraments, is a community celebration. When possible, celebrating it in the context of parish, home, or family is encouraged. The sick person has a better opportunity to appreciate the prayers and symbols of the rite when in her or his worshiping community.

Anyone who is hospitalized or homebound can receive the sacrament of the anointing of the sick as well. When possible, family, friends, or representatives of the parish community may be present.

Sickness Involves More Than Bodily Illness
Tensions, fear, and anxiety about the future affect not only our minds but also our bodies. These illnesses can be serious. They can move us to ask for the healing touch of Christ in the sacrament of anointing.

Persons suffering from addictions can be anointed as can those who suffer from mental illness. Christ's power can be invoked in the sacrament when anxiety precedes surgery. The spouse or principal caregiver of an ill person may be anointed when he or she, too, is seriously affected by the illness.

Anointing Heals Us Through Faith
Does it work? Will I experience healing? Yes, healing always takes place. However, that healing isn't restricted to mere physical healing.

When our attention is directed toward physical illness, it's natural to think of the effects of the sacrament in terms of physical healing. Sacraments, however, are celebrations of faith, expressions of who we are before God.

The healing following the anointing of the sick is a different kind of healing than a medicinal treatment or surgical intervention. Sacraments are acts of faith; they grace the whole person—body, soul, and spirit. The blessing over the oil for anointing asks God to "send the power of your Holy Spirit, the Consoler, into this precious oil….Make this oil a remedy for all who are anointed with it; heal them in body, in soul, and in spirit, and deliver them from every affliction" (*Pastoral Care of the Sick*, 123). The sick person may or may not experience physical healing, but he or she is strengthened spiritually in time of need. Reassurance of God's care and that of the community brings comfort and peace to the ailing and anxious.

Value in Suffering

"Christians feel and experience pain as do all other people; yet their faith helps them to grasp more deeply the mystery of suffering and to bear their pain with greater courage. From Christ's words they know that sickness has meaning and value for their own salvation and the salvation of the world. They also know that Christ, who during his life often visited and healed the sick, loves them in their illness."

Pastoral Care of the Sick, 1

Value in Suffering

Read or refer to section 1501 of the *Catechism*, which asserts that illness can help a person to "discern in his life what is not essential" and to "turn toward that which is." Ask participants, "When has illness, suffering, or pain caused you to rethink your life? What factors played a part in your making major changes or decisions?"

Journey of Faith for Adults, Catechumenate Leader Guide

In this sacrament, we pray that the sick be healed in body, soul, and spirit. God alone knows what kind of healing the sick need most: healing a wound, converting fear into courage, lessening loneliness, turning confusion into insight.

The sacrament of anointing helps us gain insight into the meaning of human suffering. While it doesn't remove the mystery of human suffering, its celebration gives us a window into the mystery of a loving God who raises up the crucified Son to display his victorious wounds, sitting triumphant at the Father's right hand.

- When have you been healed physically, spiritually, or emotionally?
- How did your healing come about?
- What did you learn from your experience of suffering?

How Is the Anointing of the Sick Celebrated Today?

Since this sacrament focuses on the healing of body, spirit, and soul, those who will be anointed are encouraged to celebrate the other sacrament of healing—the sacrament of penance and reconciliation—prior to the anointing service. The rite of anointing may be celebrated within Mass or outside of Mass with a Liturgy of the Word that instructs those gathered on the deeper Christian meaning of sickness and suffering and to celebrate the sacrament in renewed faith.

The *laying on of hands*, an ancient Christian gesture, symbolizes and confers the special grace of the Holy Spirit.

The priest *anoints* the forehead and hands of the sick person with the *oil of the sick*. The forehead is anointed as a reminder of the sign of the cross traced on the forehead at baptism. As the priest anoints the forehead, he says, "Through this holy anointing may the Lord in his love and mercy help you with the grace of the Holy Spirit."

The anointing of the hands signifies the Holy Spirit meeting us in our personal situation. As the hands are anointed, the priest prays, "May the Lord who frees you from sin save you and raise you up." The person answers, "Amen."

How Often Can Someone Be Anointed?

Some need this sacramental grace to sustain them at a psychological or emotional level. Some need grace for an actual cure. Others, because of the extreme nature of the illness, need the grace to enter more deeply into the suffering of Christ.

This sacrament can be requested any time a person has an illness that might lead to death, is facing surgery, suffering the ailments of advanced age, or entering a new phase of illness. It's not unusual for a person to celebrate this sacrament more than once.

Prior to the Second Vatican Council (1962–65), anointing of the sick was used mostly for those close to death. The council restored this sacrament to its original purpose, changing its name from *extreme unction* (final anointing) to *anointing of the sick*.

How Is the Anointing of the Sick Celebrated Today?

Review the steps in the sacrament (rite). Compare the modern-day symbols (blessed oil) and actions (laying on of hands) with those of the early Church.

How Often Can Someone Be Anointed?

Emphasize that both catechumens and candidates may request the sacrament if it is needed. Invite sponsors and team members to share their stories or experiences, such as when a close friend or relative requested it.

The Sacrament of Anointing of the Sick

Provide participants with a list of parish contacts in these ministries. Some participants or sponsors may have careers in the fields of health care, hospice care, or psychiatric care and be able to address these questions directly or even share with the RCIA group. Encourage them to consider how their talents might be used to serve the Church.

Remind everyone present that most of us comfort, nurture, and assist the sick and suffering already—either as a parent of young children, relative of an elderly or disabled person, or supportive friend or neighbor. Even without physical proximity or the ability to physically, emotionally, or spiritually heal, we can call on Jesus' healing touch through prayer, the saints, and personal cards or messages.

How Can I Participate in Christ's Healing Ministry?

While priests are the only ones who can sacramentally anoint the sick, ministry to the sick is a concern of the entire Christian community. Talk to a Catholic health-care professional, a hospital or hospice chaplain, a member of your parish who takes Communion to the sick and homebound, or someone who visits the sick in nursing homes. Ask them about their ministry and how it addresses the total person—body, soul, and spirit.

Find out how your local parish supports its sick members through service and prayer. Then answer the following questions in your journal:

- *How is God calling me to join in his care of the sick in my community?*
- *Who do I personally know who may benefit from a visit, card, or meal? Commit to reaching out to this person in the coming week.*

Journey of Faith for Adults, Catechumenate Leader Guide

Closing Prayer

Ask the participants to silently reflect on ways in which, or places where, they may need healing. Invite them to focus on one aspect of their life for this prayer. Spend a moment or two in quiet meditation, then ask each person to mention a loved one in need of spiritual, physical, or mental healing. To conclude, pray the Our Father together.

Take-home

Remind participants to interview people as needed for the lesson's activity and to record all their thoughts, responses, and findings in their journal this week.

The Sacrament of Anointing of the Sick

C8: The Sacrament of Matrimony

Catechism: 1533–35; 1601–66

Objectives

Participants will…

- discover ways in which the sacrament of marriage mirrors the love of God, paschal mystery, and unity of the Holy Trinity.
- describe marriage as an expression and sign of God's love (self-giving, forgiving, faithful, lifelong, intimate, unifying, and creative).
- recognize Catholic teachings on marriage, family, and human sexuality, including the difference between an annulment and civil divorce.

Leader Meditation

Colossians 3:12–17

How does this passage encourage us to treat one another? Consider your own attitudes toward marriage and the difficulties you may have encountered in relationships. When have you witnessed the special marital grace that is available to husbands and wives? Are there times in your life or the lives of other married people in which you witnessed God's grace active in moments of great joy, sorrow, or confusion?

Related *Catholic Updates*

- "Sacrament of Marriage: Sign of Faithful Love" (C9605A)
- "The Spirituality of Marriage: Becoming Signs of God's Love" (C9705A)
- "Human Sexuality: 'Wonderful Gift' and 'Awesome Responsibility'" (C9208A)
- "The How and Why of Natural Family Planning" (C8506A)

Leader Preparation

- Read the lesson, this lesson plan, the opening Scripture, and the *Catechism* sections.
- Be familiar with the following vocabulary terms: chastity, natural family planning. Definitions are provided in this guide's glossary.
- Be aware of any participants who are divorced, separated, or struggling with a troubled marriage, as well as those engaged to be married. Refer anyone in an irregular marriage or needing an annulment to your pastor or diocesan ministry, and engaged couples to the marriage-preparation coordinator. If appropriate, offer to employ the support of sponsors and spiritual directors.
- Invite parishioners who are active in a marriage ministry (preparation, enrichment, or counseling) to speak to the participants about the sacrament, spirituality, and vocation of marriage during this session. Encourage all spouses to attend.

Welcome

Greet each person warmly as he or she arrives. Allow individuals to introduce their spouse or special guest. Solicit questions or comments about the previous session and/or share new information and findings. Begin promptly.

Opening Scripture

Colossians 3:12–17

Light the candle and read the passage aloud. Talk about the virtues necessary to maintain healthy relationships, whether they are between spouses, coworkers, classmates, or friends. Emphasize the virtues advocated by St. Paul: "kindness, humility, gentleness, and patience," as well as mercy, peace, and above all, love. Ask, "What traits and skills do you rely on to build better and loving connections?"

> The matrimonial covenant, by which a man and a woman establish between themselves a partnership of the whole of life,…has been raised by Christ the Lord to the dignity of a sacrament.
>
> CCC 1601

Journey of Faith for Adults, Catechumenate Leader Guide

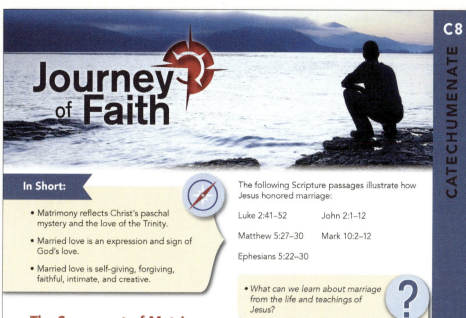

Journey of Faith

C8 CATECHUMENATE

In Short:
- Matrimony reflects Christ's paschal mystery and the love of the Trinity.
- Married love is an expression and sign of God's love.
- Married love is self-giving, forgiving, faithful, intimate, and creative.

The following Scripture passages illustrate how Jesus honored marriage:

Luke 2:41–52   John 2:1–12

Matthew 5:27–30   Mark 10:2–12

Ephesians 5:22–30

- What can we learn about marriage from the life and teachings of Jesus?

The Sacrament of Matrimony

The Catholic concept of Christian marriage involves more than holding the wedding ceremony in a church. What makes a marriage Christian isn't a Church blessing added to a legal contract.

Christian marriage is a relationship of life-giving love in which a man and a woman make the love of Christ present to each other and become a sign of the love of Christ to those around them. Through their love and faithfulness, they help each other grow in holiness.

Jesus gave the sacraments to his Church so that he could continue to touch us in our daily lives. In marriage, the relationship of the couple is the sacrament that reveals the love of God for all of us.

The Importance of Marriage

The Church didn't invent marriage. At first, there wasn't even a special Christian form of marriage. Through Jesus' teachings, the faithful realized that marriage should be appreciated as a sacred vocation. The Church continues to praise the goodness of family life and to teach that married love is a sharing in God's love.

Christians see marriage as a sacred covenant, a way of joining the shared lives of a couple with God. It's a way of living that adds richness and value to married lives—and serves as a witness of God's love.

- How might Christian marriage benefit the spouses, family, Church, and society?

CCC 1533–35; 1601–66

ADULTS

The Sacrament of Matrimony

Be particularly sensitive to the feelings of all those present as you review the lesson and discuss the topics. Even cradle Catholics struggle with these and related issues. Respond to basic questions and concerns as best as you can, but don't evade critical teachings, make judgments, or assume authority. Offer to respond to personal or emotionally charged comments outside of the session.

Invite the participants to talk about particularly good marriages that they have witnessed. Ask them, "What virtues mentioned in the reading from Colossians are present in these marriages? In what ways have these husbands and wives made Christ present to each other?"

Share these examples of Jesus' honoring marriage as needed:

- Luke 2:41–52, the Boy Jesus in the Temple, "[Jesus] said to them, 'Why were you looking for me? Did you not know that I must be in my Father's house?' But they did not understand what he said to them. He went down with them and came to Nazareth, and was obedient to them."
As a child, Christ honored and obeyed his parents, even when his words and actions baffled or frustrated them.

- John 2:1–12, the wedding at Cana, "His mother said to the servers, 'Do whatever he tells you.' …Jesus told them, 'Fill the jars with water.'… And when the headwaiter tasted the water that had become wine, without knowing where it came from…, the headwaiter called the bridegroom…"
Jesus performed his first miracle and "revealed his glory" during a wedding celebration.

- Matthew 5:27–30 "I say to you, everyone who looks at a woman with lust has already committed adultery with her in his heart." Jesus discouraged divorce and warned against lust.

- Mark 10:2–12 "But from the beginning of creation, 'God made them male and female. For this reason a man shall leave his father and mother [and be joined to his wife], and the two shall become one flesh.' …Therefore what God has joined together, no human being must separate." Jesus described the marital union as permanent, natural, and sacred. He also established the institution as intrinsically connected to the conjugal act, that is, between one man and one woman.

- Ephesians 5:22–30 "For the husband is head of his wife just as Christ is head of the church, he himself the savior of the body…. Husbands, love your wives, even as Christ loved the church and handed himself over for her to sanctify her…So [also] husbands should love their wives as their own bodies."
St. Paul relates marriage to a loving and redeeming sacrifice, particularly to the paschal mystery.

The Sacrament of Matrimony

Signs of God's Love

Emphasize that Catholic teachings on marriage, family, and sexuality are not arbitrary but rooted in Christ, Scripture, and natural law (God's design).

Provide these examples if needed (see also above): marriage as between one man and one woman and procreative (Genesis 1:27–28); marriage as holy and permanent (Genesis 2:24).

Note that marriage is unique from the other sacraments in that the *spouses*—not an ordained minister—confer the Spirit's grace upon each other. The great responsibility to perform that act and to receive that gift fully is one reason why Catholic marriage-preparation programs are so involved. Other churches and faiths have seen this wisdom and begun to follow suit. Invite married participants and sponsors to share favorite and valued aspects of their preparations for marriage.

Signs of God's Love

We understand the true nature of married love only when we realize that it comes from God, who is love. Catholics believe that a marriage between two baptized Christians is sacramental—a sign of Christ.

In the rite of marriage, the Church recognizes "the exchange of consent between the spouses to be the indispensable element that 'makes the marriage'....'The partners mutually give themselves to each other': 'I take you to be my wife'—'I take you to be my husband.' This consent that binds the spouses to each other finds its fulfillment in the two 'becoming one flesh'" (CCC 1626–27). This consent must be freely given.

The couple may exchange rings as a sign of their love and fidelity to each other and as a reminder of God's never-ending love and faithfulness.

A married couple makes Christ present to each other. That's why the ministers of the sacrament of matrimony are the husband and wife.

> "We have come to know and to believe in the love God has for us. God is love, and whoever remains in love remains in God and God in him."
>
> 1 John 4:16

Characteristics of Love

Married couples find many opportunities for learning acceptance, tolerance, and forgiveness. In a Scripture passage used at many Christian weddings, St. Paul offers several characteristics of love: "Love is patient, love is kind…" (see 1 Corinthians 13:4–8). We find additional definitions of love throughout Scripture as God reveals his love for his people. Based on St. John's assertion that "God is love" (1 John 4:16), we learn from God's love how to love each other.

*Ephesians 5
Proverbs 31*

Love Is Self-giving

Founded on God's giving of himself, married love is based on giving. Total loving means total giving of oneself "freely and without reservation" (*Rite of Marriage*). Married love is a choice to love our spouse unconditionally and requires sacrifice for the good of the other. In choosing to love, we make the decision to give without resentment, forgive completely, and put the other's needs before our own. Two people joined in marriage become one as they share their unique gifts for the sake of the other.

- When have you witnessed or shared self-giving love?

Love Is Forgiving

God's mercy and forgiveness is reflected in the way a couple reconciles differences, forgives hurts, and heals each other. Willingness to reconcile again and again is an example of the desire for reconciliation God has for us.

- When has willingness to forgive or to ask for forgiveness strengthened your relationship?

Love Is Faithful

A couple is asked on their wedding day, "Will you love and honor each other as man and wife for the rest of your lives?" (*Rite of Marriage*). This promise isn't just for days that go well or seasons of life that are easy. It's a lifelong commitment that doesn't end.

God's faithfulness is evident in the commitment a couple makes to love each other for a lifetime. It means affirmation instead of criticism, openness instead of dismissiveness, communication instead of silence, collaboration instead of demands. Modeled on God's faithfulness, married love accepts, affirms, looks for the good, and encourages personal growth.

- What married couple models faithful love? How might you affirm or thank them?

Love Is Faithful

Emphasize that marriage is symbolic of our Lord's faithfulness to his Church. Remind participants of the many instances in Scripture and Church history when God's people abandoned the law and covenant. Despite all this, God's presence, truth, and the fullness of revelation remained within the community. Ask, perhaps hypothetically, what it would mean or be like had God not sent Christ or Christ not died for us.

Journey of Faith for Adults, Catechumenate Leader Guide

"they had so much love that 9 mon later they named it"

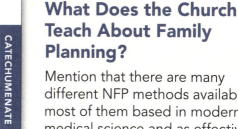

Love Is Intimate
God's love is passionate, joyful, and intimate, qualities reflected in a couple's passion for each other. The intimacy enjoyed in marriage is sexual, emotional, and spiritual. The marital embrace expresses the love of husband and wife and also makes their love grow. Sexual relations in marriage are a way to enrich each other through mutual self-giving. Their love makes them not two persons but one body. Married love that leads to growth in intimacy mirrors the love God has for us.

> • How are couples called to be intimate beyond the physical? What might spiritual intimacy look like?

Love Is Creative
Sharing in God's creative love, a couple is privileged to share in the most exalted part of God's creative work—the creation of another human being. Their generosity and love is a reflection of the Creator's love.

An essential dimension of marriage is openness to fertility and children. This means much more than the act of conception; it's the encouragement and support given to each other during the raising of children. Christian couples must be willing to bring life through each other and mutually share in the work of nurturing that life to adulthood.

The fruitfulness of marriage isn't limited to children. If a couple is unable to have children, "their marriage can radiate a fruitfulness of charity, of hospitality, and of sacrifice" (CCC 1654).

The sexual difference and complementarity of man and woman are part of God's design. Based on its understanding of God's design and will, the Catholic Church teaches that marriage is to be between one man and one woman.

Love Is Oneness
There is strength and beauty in a couple whose members are truly one. Each person is distinct, yet together they're a more complete whole. God is best revealed in marriage because God is relationship. In the blending of two into one flesh, we can catch a glimpse of the unity and mystery of the Holy Trinity.

Couples give flesh to Christ's love through intimacy and belonging. The Church and the community have a responsibility to help all married couples live out their vocation and covenant. One way the Church does this is through marriage-preparation and enrichment programs.

What Does the Church Teach About Divorce

Jesus revealed God's intention for married love: "A man shall leave his father and mother [and be joined to his wife], and the two shall become one flesh.' So they are no longer two but one flesh. Therefore what God has joined together, no human being must separate" (Mark 10:7–9).

Catholics believe a sacramental marriage between Christians can never be dissolved. Although Christians may get a civil divorce, the Church still considers the couple to be married. They cannot remarry in the Church without a decree of nullity, commonly called an annulment.

Divorced Catholics who haven't remarried remain full members of the Church. Those who have remarried outside of the Church are encouraged to seek an annulment through a process many find both healing and merciful. If an annulment is granted, marriage within the Church is again possible.

An annulment isn't a Catholic divorce. It's an official Church recognition that the marriage wasn't a true marriage—*not a sacrament*—in the first place. A decree of nullity in no way affects the legitimacy of children.

What Does the Church Teach About Family Planning?

Mention that there are many different NFP methods available, most of them based in modern medical science and as effective, if not more so, as artificial contraceptives and reproductive technologies. Within a loving marriage, these practices can take on a spiritual dimension and become much more than a means of observing a couple's fertility or regulating pregnancy.

Refer any interested participant or couple to a local NFP provider. The marriage-prep coordinator at your parish may assist you in gathering details and contact information.

What does the Church teach about divorce?

Emphasize that no marriage is perfect or without some difficulty or suffering. Occasional conflict and ups and downs are part of even the best relationships. Remind those present that if both parties are open to love and mercy, all conflicts, trials, and injuries can be overcome. *With God, all things are possible* (Matthew 19:26; Mark 10:27; Luke 1:37; 18:27).

Clarify, if necessary, that the Church never intends a spouse to remain in an unhealthy or unsafe situation. It recognizes the necessity of separation, even civil divorce, in certain situations but maintains a preference for reconciliation and that the sacramental bond is still intact. The Spirit's power is above human ability.

Explain, if necessary, that a marriage between two unbaptized persons is valid but not sacramental in the eyes of the Church. For this reason, divorced individuals who wish to remarry in the Church need an annulment from this union.

The Sacrament of Matrimony

saying "yes"

CATECHUMENATE — JOURNEY OF FAITH

Natural Family Planning

Christ calls us all to lead lives of **chastity** according to our state in life. Being chaste means we "reserve for marriage the expressions of affection that belong to married love" (CCC 2348–50). Within Christian marriage, a couple's sexual expression of love is to be both exclusive and open to the dual love-giving (unitive) and life-giving (procreative) aspects of God's design for the sexual expression of love.

The Catholic Church understands that couples may wish to space the births of children and may, for good reason, choose to limit the number of children they have. To do so, couples are encouraged to use various methods of **Natural Family Planning** (NFP).

NFP methods instruct and support the couple in reading and interpreting the biological signs of fertility and in applying this knowledge to achieve or postpone conception. No physical or chemical barrier is used to try to prevent pregnancy, allowing the total gift of self, including one's fertility, to be shared through a couple's lovemaking. These methods are completely natural and highly effective.

"NFP 'isn't just biological; it has to do with the unity of the whole person: body and spirit. It's about spouses learning the language of fertility and then living their marriages by it. It allows couples to be subject to one another out of reverence for Christ. That way, when their bodies say, "I love you," they're all the more sure their hearts mean it.'"

Fletcher Doyle in
Natural Family Planning: Key to Intimacy

- What does being chaste mean in your state in life?

Discuss the following questions with your spouse (if you're married) or married friends (if you're single). Record any insights you gain in your journal.

- How does the Catholic teaching about marriage challenge you? Why?
- How will you respond to this challenge?

Journey of Faith for Adults: Catechumenate, C8 (826245)
Imprimi Potest: Stephen T. Rehrauer, CSsR, Provincial, Denver Province, the Redemptorists.
Imprimatur: "In accordance with CIC 827, permission to publish has been granted on May 26, 2016, by the Most Reverend Edward M. Rice, Auxiliary Bishop, Archdiocese of St. Louis. Permission to publish is an indication that nothing contrary to Church teaching is contained in this work. It does not imply any endorsement of the opinions expressed in the publication, nor is any liability assumed by this permission."
Journey of Faith © 1993, 2005, 2016 Liguori Publications, Liguori, MO 63057. To order, visit Liguori.org or call 800-325-9521. Liguori Publications, a nonprofit corporation, is an apostolate of the Redemptorists. To learn more about the Redemptorists, visit Redemptorists.com. All rights reserved. No part of this publication may be reproduced, distributed, stored, transmitted, or posted in any form by any means without prior written permission.
Contributing writers: Kathy Heskin, Fr. Oscar Lukefahr, CM, and Fr. Christopher Gaffney, CSsR. Editors of 2016 Journey of Faith: Denise Bossert, Julia DiSalvo, and Joan McKamey. Design: Lorena Mitre Jimenez. Images: Shutterstock. Unless noted, Scripture texts in this work are taken from the *New American Bible*, revised edition. © 2010, 1991, 1986, 1970 Confraternity of Christian Doctrine, Washington, D.C., and are used by permission of the copyright owner. All Rights Reserved. No part of the *New American Bible* may be reproduced in any form without permission in writing from the copyright owner. Excerpts from English translation of the *Catechism of the Catholic Church* for the United States of America © 1994 United States Catholic Conference, Inc.—Libreria Editrice Vaticana; English translation of the *Catechism of the Catholic Church*: Modifications from the Editio Typica © 1997 United States Catholic Conference, Inc.—Libreria Editrice Vaticana. *Natural Family Planning: Key to Intimacy* © 2013 Liguori Publications. Compliant with *The Roman Missal*, Third Edition.
Printed in the United States of America. 20 19 18 17 16 / 5 4 3 2 1 Third Edition

LIGUORI PUBLICATIONS
A Redemptorist Ministry

Journey of Faith for Adults, Catechumenate Leader Guide

Journaling

Encourage participants to respond to the journaling prompts and many of the lesson's questions in their journal. Married or engaged participants should share their responses with their spouse or fiancé(e); single participants may share them with their sponsors.

Closing Prayer

Ask participants to silently call to mind married couples who are or have been important in their lives, as well as spouses who are struggling or need support. Then invite them to reflect on how they may become more perfect reflections of God's love in all their relationships, particularly within marriage. Ask God to grant the husbands and wives present the necessary graces to embrace their vocation. Conclude with a meditative reading of 1 Corinthians 13.

Take-home

Have participants consider ways in which they can support the sacrament and institution of marriage in their families, communities, and society. Encourage them to take at least one step toward a goal this week.

The Sacrament of Matrimony

C9: The Sacrament of Holy Orders

Catechism: 1536–1600

Objectives

Participants will...

- distinguish between the three distinct orders (degrees) of deacon, priest, and bishop.
- identify the roles of each of these callings and recognize how they are rooted in Scripture, Christ, and the early Church.
- recall the essential signs and steps of the sacrament (rite), specifically the laying on of hands.

Leader Meditation

Mark 10:43–45

Reflect on Jesus' message: that to serve others is to serve God. As an RCIA leader, you are serving God by teaching the men and women under your guidance. Ask yourself, "Do I humble myself for their sake? What gifts can I offer for their betterment?" Pray for the wisdom and grace to serve them well.

Related *Catholic Updates*

- "Sacrament of Holy Orders: Priesthood in Transition" (C9707A)
- "Father, Sister, Brother, Deacon: Is God Calling Me?" (C1010A)

Leader Preparation

- Read the lesson, this lesson plan, the opening Scripture, and the *Catechism* sections. Review inquiry lesson Q12: *Who Shepherds the Church?* if necessary.
- Be familiar with the following vocabulary terms: common priesthood, miter, crosier, paten, chalice, ordination. Definitions are provided in this guide's glossary.
- Make sure a deacon or priest attends this session so that he can speak directly and personally to the sacrament and his vocation.
- Obtain a recording of "Here I Am, Lord" by Dan Schutte (New Dawn Music) or "Here I Am" by Rory Cooney (NALR) for the closing prayer.

Welcome

Greet each person as he or she arrives. Check for supplies and immediate needs. Solicit questions or comments about the previous session and/or share new information and findings. Invite the priest or deacon to open the session with a general blessing, or together make the sign of the cross.

Opening Scripture

Mark 10:43–45

Light the candle and read the passage aloud. Talk about the powerful message that Jesus gave his apostles. Emphasize that service to others was not a mere suggestion—it was a command! We serve God best by serving other people. Have the participants reflect on these questions: "Who can I serve and bring closer to Christ's Church? Who serves me?"

> The sacrament of Holy Orders communicates a "sacred power" which is none other than that of Christ. The exercise of this authority must therefore be measured against the model of Christ, who by love made himself the least and the servant of all.
>
> CCC 1551

Journey of Faith for Adults, Catechumenate Leader Guide

C9 · CATECHUMENATE · ADULTS

In Short:
- The three orders in the sacrament of holy orders are bishop, priest, deacon.
- The roots of this sacrament are in the acts of Jesus and the early Church.
- Laying on of hands with a prayer of consecration is the essential sign of holy orders.

The Sacrament of Holy Orders

Archbishop Óscar Romero's homilies defending the rights of the poor were broadcast by radio. On March 23, 1980, people throughout El Salvador heard him condemn the military's repressive actions against the poor. The next morning, an assassin killed Archbishop Romero as he celebrated Mass.

A prisoner had escaped from a concentration camp in Auschwitz. In retaliation, the Nazi commandant chose ten other prisoners to be starved to death. One of the men chosen sobbed, "My wife, my children!" Fr. Maximilian Kolbe stepped forward, saying, "I want to die in place of this prisoner." His request was granted.

As the early Church grew, the apostles needed assistants and chose seven men "filled with the Spirit and wisdom" to help them minister to the people. Among these first deacons was Stephen, who was stoned to death for refusing to stop preaching the word of God (see Acts 6–7).

These men are powerful examples of living servants of Christ and the Church. Through baptism, God calls all of us to lives of humble service and sacrifice. Some men are called to serve the Church as ordained ministers.

The Common Priesthood

All the baptized share in the priesthood of Christ. God calls us to "consecrate the world itself to God" in the **common priesthood** of the faithful. Through our good works, prayers, occupations, recreation, and hardships, we both serve others and lead them to Christ" (Dogmatic Constitution on the Church [Lumen Gentium], 34).

"Like living stones, let yourselves be built into a spiritual house to be a holy priesthood to offer spiritual sacrifices acceptable to God through Jesus Christ."

1 Peter 2:5

"The faithful indeed, by virtue of their royal priesthood, share in the offering of the Eucharist. They exercise that priesthood, too, by the reception of the sacraments, by prayer and thanksgiving, by the witness of a holy life, self-denial and active charity."

Lumen Gentium 10

- How does my life give praise and honor to God?

CCC 1536–1600

The Sacrament of Holy Orders

Invite participants to share their reactions to the stories of Blessed Óscar Romero, St. Maximilian Kolbe, and St. Stephen, all martyrs.

Ask participants and sponsors to describe their experiences with the Catholic clergy. Say, "What made these men seem ordinary or extraordinary?"

The Common Priesthood

Make sure participants understand the distinction between the common priesthood of all believers and the ordained priesthood, which is seen in the use of *presbyters* in Acts 15:6, 23.

Read this quote from the *Catechism*: "The ministerial priesthood is at the service of the common priesthood. It is directed at the unfolding of the baptismal grace of all Christians" (CCC 1547). Invite responses from the participants.

Ordained to Serve

Emphasize that the sacred power of holy orders stresses faithful, dedicated service to the people of God. Remind participants that priests are human and subject to human weakness. Jesus Christ is the only perfect priest.

Share these responses to the passages from Hebrews as needed:

- Hebrews 4:14–16 "We do not have a high priest who is unable to sympathize with our weaknesses, but one who has similarly been tested in every way, yet without sin."
  Jesus is a true priest in that he has suffered all things, sacrificed all things, and served God and others perfectly.

- Hebrews 5:1–4, 10 "He is able to deal patiently with the ignorant and erring, for he himself is beset by weakness and so, for this reason, must make sin offerings for himself as well as for the people."
  Jesus is fully human, yet the only person without sin (except his mother Mary). No priest on earth could offer the Mass and sacraments without the power of Christ.

- Hebrews 7:23–28 "He, because he remains forever, has a priesthood that does not pass away. Therefore, he is always able to save those who approach God through him… [He sacrificed] once for all when he offered himself."
  The reign of our Lord is everlasting. The life and salvation he brings is eternal.

- Hebrews 10:11–14 "This one offered one sacrifice for sins, and took his seat forever at the right hand of God; now he waits until his enemies are made his footstool."
  Jesus' sacrifice achieved complete victory over evil, sin, and death. Therefore he lives and reigns in heaven with God the Father.

Laying on of Hands

Review the steps and symbols in the rite. Invite the priest or deacon to share stories or photos of his ordination and a brief witness of his call.

Review this *Catechism* quote, which details the additional rites. They "symbolically express and complete the mystery accomplished: for bishop and priest, an anointing with holy chrism, a sign of the special anointing of the Holy Spirit who makes their ministry fruitful; giving the book of the Gospels, the ring, the miter, and the crosier to the bishop as the sign of his apostolic mission to proclaim the Word of God, of his fidelity to the Church, the bride of Christ, and his office as shepherd of the Lord's flock; presentation to the priest of the paten and chalice, 'the offering of the holy people' which he is called to present to God; giving the book of the Gospels to the deacon who has just received the mission to proclaim the Gospel of Christ" (CCC 1574).

Share the answer to the lesson's question if necessary: *The laying*

CATECHUMENATE — JOURNEY OF FAITH

Ordained to Serve

Every community or organization needs leaders—including the Church. In Old Testament times, God designated the tribe of Levi for liturgical services. Their role was "to act on behalf of men in relation to God, to offer gifts and sacrifices for sins" (CCC 1539).

The sacrament of holy orders establishes bishops, priests, and deacons as official Church leaders. Through this sacrament, men are ordained "to serve in the name and in the person of Christ the Head in the midst of the community" (CCC 1591).

Holy orders "confers a sacred power for the service of the faithful. The ordained ministers exercise their service for the People of God by teaching, divine worship and pastoral governance" (CCC 1592). For example, ordained ministers teach by preaching, living as examples of faith, and providing for faith formation. They practice divine worship by administering sacraments and leading blessings and prayers. They govern through diocesan or parish administration.

Read these passages from the Letter to the Hebrews. They teach us about Christ as the true priest:

Hebrews 4:14–16   Hebrews 5:1–4, 10
Hebrews 7:23–28   Hebrews 10:11–14

- From these passages, what do you understand of the priest's role?
- What characteristics are shared by the ordained and common priesthood?

Instituted By Christ

The priesthood became perfected in Christ, who sacrificed himself once for all time. Knowing his time on earth was limited, Jesus sent out his apostles to preach and baptize (see Matthew 10) and gave them the power to heal and forgive sins (see Mark 6:1–3; John 20:23). At the Last Supper, Jesus gave his apostles the power to celebrate the Eucharist. The Twelve served the Church as the first bishops.

Laying on of Hands

The laying on of hands by the bishop, with a prayer of consecration, is the essential rite in the sacrament of holy orders. In the prayer, the bishop asks "God for the outpouring of the Holy Spirit and his gifts proper to the ministry to which the candidate is being ordained" (CCC 1573). Ordination "confers a gift of the Holy Spirit that permits the exercise of a 'sacred power' which can come only from Christ himself through his Church" (CCC 1592).

Some additional rites include an anointing with chrism (bishop and priest), presentation of ring, **miter**, and **crosier** (bishop), giving the *Book of the Gospels* (bishop, priest, deacon), and presentation of **paten** and **chalice** (priest).

> "Set an example for those who believe, in speech, conduct, love, faith, and purity. Until I arrive, attend to the reading, exhortation, and teaching. Do not neglect the gift you have, which was conferred on you…with the imposition of hands."
>
> 1 Timothy 4:12–14

- In what other sacraments is the laying on of hands a sign? How is it used in each?

Confirmation anointing

Journey of Faith for Adults, Catechumenate Leader Guide

Leading the Early Church

As the Church spread and grew, those blessed with strong faith and the ability to preach and teach became leaders. Their position was set apart by the laying on of hands and the calling down of the Holy Spirit (2 Timothy 1:6–7). This marked the beginning of formal **ordination**, the sacramental act that integrates a man into the order of bishops, priests, or deacons, making him an official minister. While everyone could proclaim the word and witness to the faith through the common priesthood, only those in the *ordained priesthood* had the power to preach in the assembly, celebrate the Eucharist, and guide the faith community.

This tradition continues today in the sacrament of holy orders. The bishops, successors of the apostles, confer (hand or pass on) orders to other men who then become bishops, priests, and deacons.

> "Holy Orders is the sacrament through which the mission entrusted by Christ to his apostles continues to be exercised in the Church until the end of time."
>
> CCC 1536

What Are the Degrees of Holy Orders?

Bishop
The office of bishop is traced to Christ's commissioning the apostles as the first leaders of the faithful. Bishops lead the local Church as Christ's representatives. Each bishop ensures the unity of his local Church with the universal Church.

As the principal teacher in his diocese, the bishop sees that the truths of the Catholic faith and the principles of morality are taught correctly. As first among preachers, he speaks in the name of Christ. When he visits a parish or celebrates a sacrament, he represents the universal Church. Our principal bishop is the pope, the bishop of Rome. A bishop can officiate at all seven sacraments.

Priest
In the early Church, the bishops ministered to everyone. As the number of believers grew, the bishops were no longer able to care for all of them. Therefore, they ordained men to act in their place. These men were the first priests.

A priest is ordained to serve in the name of the bishop and called to preach by word and action. He is the leader of worship and a sign of Christ's presence among the people. He is to take on the image of the Good Shepherd and guide his flock.

Priests can celebrate the sacraments of baptism, Eucharist, penance, and anointing of the sick, and can be the official witness at weddings. He may celebrate confirmation with the bishop's permission.

Deacon
The word *deacon* comes from the Greek for "servant" or "helper." Deacons are ordained for the threefold service "of the liturgy, of the word, and of charity to the people of God" (*LG* 29). Deacons may proclaim the word by reading the Gospel and preaching the homily at Mass. They may assist the celebrant at Mass, distribute the Eucharist, perform baptisms, officiate at weddings and funeral services, lead prayer, preach, and teach. The focus of the deacon's ministry is charity: caring for the community, especially those in need.

There are two types of deacons. The transitional diaconate is the step before ordination as a priest. A single or married man may be ordained as a permanent deacon. If a permanent deacon is single or if his wife dies, he must remain unmarried.

> "In the ecclesial service of the ordained minister, it is Christ himself who is present to his Church as Head of his Body, shepherd of his flock, high priest of the redemptive sacrifice, Teacher of Truth."
>
> CCC 1548

- What are some characteristics of a good leader?
- Which of these traits do you think are most important in an ordained minister? Why?

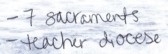

on of hands is used in confirmation and anointing. For confirmation, refer back to lesson C4. In holy orders, the laying on of hands is a reminder that this role and authority is passed down from Jesus through the disciples and that the men being ordained now share in this ministry and authority.

Leading the Early Church

Emphasize the meaning and importance of the ministerial priesthood. Recall that Jesus sent the apostles out to do what he had done. Ask participants, "What responsibilities does the honor of being sent bring with it?"

What Are the Degrees of Holy Orders?

Encourage participants to learn more about the clergy who serve their parish and diocese. Some church websites provide short bios of the staff and leaders. Attending parish events may allow them to meet the pastor and parishioners in a social setting. If there's time, the priest or deacon may share a little more about himself with those present.

Remind participants that the degrees of holy orders and Church hierarchy were discussed in lesson Q12: *Who Shepherds the Church?* Review that material with them as needed.

The Sacrament of Holy Orders

Why Celibacy?

Distinguish celibacy from chastity, which was discussed in the previous lesson (C8: *The Sacrament of Matrimony*). Clarify, if necessary, that a celibate man or woman is not asexual: Everyone has a biological gender, and human sexuality is much more than acts of intercourse. Remind them that unmarried adults are similarly called to abstain from sexual acts.

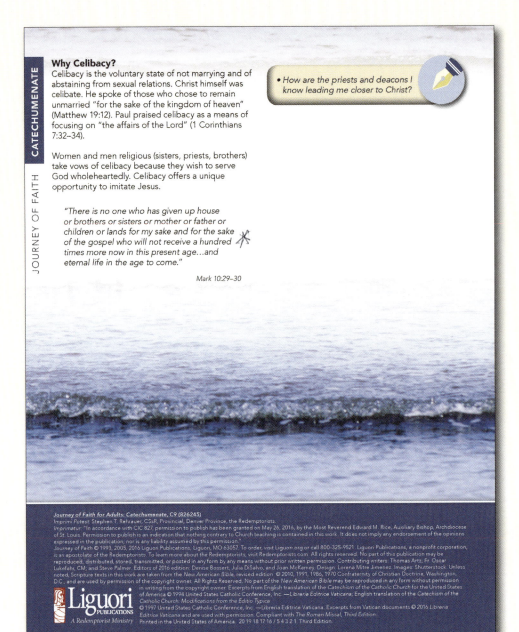

Why Celibacy?

Celibacy is the voluntary state of not marrying and of abstaining from sexual relations. Christ himself was celibate. He spoke of those who chose to remain unmarried "for the sake of the kingdom of heaven" (Matthew 19:12). Paul praised celibacy as a means of focusing on "the affairs of the Lord" (1 Corinthians 7:32–34).

Women and men religious (sisters, priests, brothers) take vows of celibacy because they wish to serve God wholeheartedly. Celibacy offers a unique opportunity to imitate Jesus.

> "There is no one who has given up house or brothers or sisters or mother or father or children or lands for my sake and for the sake of the gospel who will not receive a hundred times more now in this present age…and eternal life in the age to come."
>
> Mark 10:29–30

- How are the priests and deacons I know leading me closer to Christ?

Journey of Faith for Adults, Catechumenate Leader Guide

Journaling

Have participants reflect on their vocations. What has God called them to do? How can they serve the Church and support the ministerial priesthood? Do they know anyone who may be called to holy orders or the religious life? Have participants respond to the lesson's prompt and this question in their journals: *How can I share the faith and reach those the ordained priest cannot?*

Closing Prayer

Pray for any special intentions, then ask the participants to sit comfortably and meditate on the lyrics of the hymn they are about to hear. If possible, dim the lights so that the light from the candle is more visible. Conclude by playing the recording of Schutte's "Here I Am, Lord" or Cooney's "Here I Am."

Take-home

Encourage participants to make a gesture of gratitude for the ministerial priesthood this week. Suggest that they send the pastor a thank-you card, share a personal message with a member of the clergy, say a special prayer, or make a gift or act of charity to the parish, diocese, local seminary, or a religious institute.

The Sacrament of Holy Orders

C10: The People of God

Catechism: 56–64, 121–23, 128–30, 1961–64

Objectives
Participants will…
- recall major figures and events in salvation history, particularly those of the Old Testament.
- view the Israelites as our patriarchs and matriarchs in the faith and a precursor to the Church on earth.
- grasp the connection between the Old Testament (Old Covenant) and the New Testament (New Covenant).

Leader Meditation
Genesis 15:1–6

Throughout the Old Testament, we see God's ever-constant presence with and protection of the people of God. We also see the people's constant struggle between faith and fear, between faithfulness to the Lord and desire for earthly treasure. What does this passage tell you about God? About God's faithfulness? How does Scripture connect you with God's people throughout history?

Related *Catholic Update*
- "Finding Your Way Through the Old Testament" (C8911A)

Leader Preparation
- Read the lesson, this lesson plan, the opening Scripture, and the *Catechism* sections. For a more thorough review of these figures and events, read and reflect on Genesis 15—21, 24—26, and Exodus 7—16.
- Be familiar with the following vocabulary terms: Passover, exodus. Definitions are provided in this guide's glossary.
- Review lesson Q5: *The Bible* to refresh your memory of biblical history and the major sections and themes of the Old Testament, if needed.
- Obtain a video rendition of an Old Testament account, such as Abraham's near-sacrifice, Joseph's plight and rise in Egypt, or Moses' leading out the Israelites and receiving the Ten Commandments. Prepare a short clip for the session; some docudramas and formats are already divided into episodes, scenes, or tracks.

Welcome
Greet each person as he or she arrives. Check for supplies and immediate needs. Solicit questions or comments about the previous session and/or share new information and findings. Begin promptly.

Opening Scripture
Genesis 15:1–6

Light the candle and read the passage aloud. In this reading, God rewards Abram for his faithfulness and tells him that his descendants will be as countless as the stars. Reflect on God's promise of faithfulness. Ask the participants, "How do we know that God still walks faithfully beside us today?"

Suggested responses may include the gift of faith, the words and promises of Jesus, the enduring tradition and authority of the Church, and the everyday witnesses and experiences of the saints and Christians around the world.

> The people descended from Abraham would be the trustees of the promise made to the patriarchs, the chosen people, called to prepare for that day when God would gather all his children into the unity of the Church.
>
> *CCC 60*

Journey of Faith for Adults, Catechumenate Leader Guide

C10 CATECHUMENATE

In Short:

- Salvation history recounts humanity's relationship with God, starting with Abraham.
- Old Testament figures and the Israelites are our ancestors in faith.
- Jesus fulfills the covenant God made with the Israelites in the Old Testament.

The People of God

Your journey of faith began the moment you became aware of God's presence in your life. Whether it was a dramatic conversion experience or a gradual awakening, this awareness marked a starting point in your relationship with God. But there was never a time when you were outside of God's awareness—you were fashioned in God's thought and brought to life by God's love. His love for you is nothing new.

In the Old Testament, we find a narrative of God's relationship with his people—the awakening of their awareness and accounts of their turning toward God, turning away from God, and returning to God. You may recognize your own story in these ancient ones.

- *What Old Testament stories or figures are you already familiar with?*

Abraham, Our Father in Faith

Genesis 15–21

After Adam and Eve, humanity wandered far from God. As generations passed, God slipped from the conscious thought of the people. Only a few recognized God's presence in their lives.

Among those few was Abram. God told him, "Go forth from your land, your relatives, and from your father's house to a land that I will show you" (Genesis 12:1). Leaving their home, Abram and his wife, Sarai, traveled into the unknown.

God led them to a land called Canaan. Here, God gave them new names: *Abraham*, meaning "father of many nations," and *Sarah*, meaning "princess of the people." God promised Abraham that his children and his children's children would outnumber the stars in the sky and the sands of the earth.

A new life had begun for Abraham and Sarah, one they hadn't planned for themselves. In Canaan, they prospered and grew old but remained childless. Without losing faith, Abraham and Sarah wondered if God would be true to his promise.

When they were quite old, Sarah brought forth their first and only son. Sarah's reaction at the idea of giving birth at her age was to laugh. Sarah named their son *Isaac*, which means "God's laugh." Their faith, trust in God's plan, and patience led at last to their greatest joy.

- *In what way is God leading you to new life?*

CCC 56–64; 121–123; 128–130; 1961–1964

ADULTS

C10

The People of God

List, as a group brainstorming exercise, some key figures and events in biblical history. Suggest figures candidates may know from popular Bible stories.

Emphasize the importance of studying and understanding the Hebrew Scriptures. As Christians, our own faith has deep roots in these stories. Remind participants that the Old and New Testaments together are an inspired record of our salvation history.

Abraham, Our Father in Faith

Emphasize important themes in the Hebrew Scriptures as you review each section, especially God's faithfulness despite the infidelity of the people and God's mercy and forgiveness when the people have sinned.

Play the video clip or episode after discussing the main character in the lesson. Set the scene or context beforehand and allow the viewers to respond afterward. If this will disrupt the overall session, wait until after the journaling or closing prayer. You may also assign participants the full-length feature for home viewing.

The People of God

CATECHUMENATE | JOURNEY OF FAITH

Israel in a Foreign Land

Genesis 37—45

Isaac and Rebekah's son, Jacob, the younger of twins, cheated his brother, Esau, out of their father's inheritance (see Genesis 25:19—27:44). God renamed Jacob Israel. He went on to father the leaders of the twelve tribes of Israel.

Joseph, the second-youngest of Israel's twelve sons, dreamed that his brothers bowed before him like sheaves of wheat. When he shared the dream, his brothers became angry, and some plotted to kill him. Two brothers intervened, and Joseph was sold to merchants heading for Egypt. The other brothers told their father that Joseph was dead.

The merchants sold Joseph to the Pharaoh of Egypt. After Joseph interpreted Pharaoh's dreams, the powerful ruler made Joseph second in command. Through more dreams, Joseph knew to prepare Egypt for a coming famine. During the famine, Joseph's brothers traveled to Egypt to find food. Not recognizing Joseph, his brothers bowed before him, begging for food.

When they returned to Egypt with their youngest brother, Joseph revealed himself. He forgave them and told them God had used their weakness to save them all. God had sent him to Egypt ahead of them to keep them safe during the famine. Joseph sent for his father, and the whole family of Israel settled in Egypt, where they lived well for many years.

- When have you acted selfishly, as Jacob and Joseph's brothers did?
- How did God's generous love make something good come out of your wrongdoing?

Moses: Sent to Free God's People

Exodus 2—4

As generations passed, a later Pharaoh sensed danger in the growing number of Israelites in Egypt. He enslaved them and ordered the death of every newborn Israelite male.

One Israelite mother placed her infant son in a basket and hid him in the reeds of the river. Finding the baby, Pharaoh's daughter adopted him and called him Moses. His biological mother contrived to become the baby's nurse and set about teaching him his heritage.

When Moses was grown, he killed an Egyptian who was beating an Israelite. Pharaoh heard about it and wanted Moses put to death, but Moses ran away and lived as a shepherd for many years.

One day, Moses saw a bush that burned but wasn't consumed by the fire. When he approached, a voice called out:

"Do not come near! Remove your sandals from your feet, for the place where you stand is holy ground. I am the God of your father, …the God of Abraham, the God of Isaac, and the God of Jacob."

Exodus 3:5–6

God gave Moses a mission: return to Egypt and tell Pharaoh to free his people. Moses made excuses. He wasn't great at speaking. But God showed him how to perform miracles and told him to bring along his brother, Aaron, who was a good speaker. Finally, Moses agreed.

- What excuses have you used to resist God's call to follow him?

Journey of Faith for Adults, Catechumenate Leader Guide

From Slavery to Freedom

Exodus, Deuteronomy
When Moses and Aaron delivered God's command to free the Israelites, Pharaoh laughed, and a struggle between divine and earthly power began. Egypt was struck by a series of disastrous plagues. The Pharaoh still refused to free the Israelites.

Then came the final plague. Moses had the Israelites prepare their homes by marking their doorways with lamb's blood as a sign that a family of God lived there. Seeing the blood, the angel of death would *pass over* their homes. At midnight, death took the firstborn of every Egyptian family. Pharaoh finally understood the power of God and agreed to let the Israelites go. (This event is celebrated in the Jewish feast of **Passover**.)

After centuries of slavery, the Israelites were free. They were grateful at first but soon started to complain. God gave Moses the *Ten Commandments* to guide them in right living. They wandered forty years in the wilderness as God changed their hearts and taught them to be faithful to him.

When they reached the Promised Land, their **exodus** from Egypt was over and their relationship with God had again become vital to their worship and identity.

From Judges to Kings

1 and 2 Samuel
As the years passed, the people strayed again from following God. He sent judges to rule them, but the people wanted a king. God warned them that a king wouldn't be as lenient or generous as he was.

The first king, Saul, grew jealous of the popularity of the young shepherd, David, who was well-known for killing the Philistine warrior Goliath with a sling and stones.

David became king and led Israel to prosperity. But David encountered tragedies in his personal life: his sons betrayed him, he committed adultery, and he caused the death of his lover's husband. David asked for God's forgiveness. God forgave him and promised that David's kingdom would never end and that one of his descendants "shall be a son to me" (2 Samuel 7:14). Christians believe this refers to Jesus, who was born into the line of David.

- How did God "write straight with the crooked lines" of David and others he chose to lead his people?

Split Kingdom, Prophets, and Exile

1 and 2 Kings—1 and 2 Maccabees
David's son Solomon built the Temple in Jerusalem but eventually turned away from God. After his death, the kingdom split: Israel to the north and Judah to the south. These kingdoms often warred against each other and continued to worship idols. Many prophets warned them to reform their lives and return to living the covenant made with God. The warnings of the prophets often fell on deaf ears.

The prophets' main role wasn't to predict the future but to "speak for God" on the issues of the day. The prophet *Isaiah*, however, is believed to have foretold the coming of a messiah who would bring salvation to the Israelites and people (see Isaiah 7:14, 9:6–7, 11:1–10, 49:6).

- Why didn't the people listen to the prophets? When has someone told you a truth you didn't want to hear?

Just as prophets had warned, the Babylonians conquered Israel, destroyed the Temple, and took many into exile. A small number called a "remnant" remained faithful (Zephaniah 3:12–13). They looked with hope to reconciliation with God and a return of the glory of King David's reign.

The Babylonian exile ended when the Persians conquered the Babylonians and allowed the Israelites to return to their homeland and begin rebuilding the Temple. From 63 BC, the Roman Empire extended its control over the region.

From Judges to Kings

Assist catechumens in drawing parallels between the gradual conversion of God's people and their own personal conversions. Remind all participants that the process of conversion is never really complete. Clarify that this doesn't mean sin is inevitable or membership in the Church is never achieved, but that we can always grow closer to God and discover more of his truth until we enter his kingdom and receive it in full.

Split Kingdom, Prophets, and Exile

Discuss the meaning of the word *prophet* in biblical times. Ask the participants to give examples of modern-day prophets, that is, men and women who have the vision and courage to draw us toward the truth. Reflect on the reality that the world, in both ancient and modern times, has often been unwilling to heed the words of prophets. Ask, "What challenging truths, religious or not, do you struggle to accept?"

The People of God

Complete this activity during the session. Mention, if there's time, where other Old Testament figures and stories would fit in.

———————

Share the answers with participants as needed. Additional references have been added. Extra responses may include Noah (Genesis 6–8; after Abraham) or Jonah (after Babylonian exile).

1. Abraham
2. Joseph
3. Moses
4. Exodus from Egypt (Exodus 5—15)
5. Ten Commandments (Exodus 19—20)
6. David (1 Samuel 16—18, 2 Samuel 2—7)
7. Isaiah
8. Babylonian exile (Jeremiah 39—40; 2 Kings 25; Ezra 1)

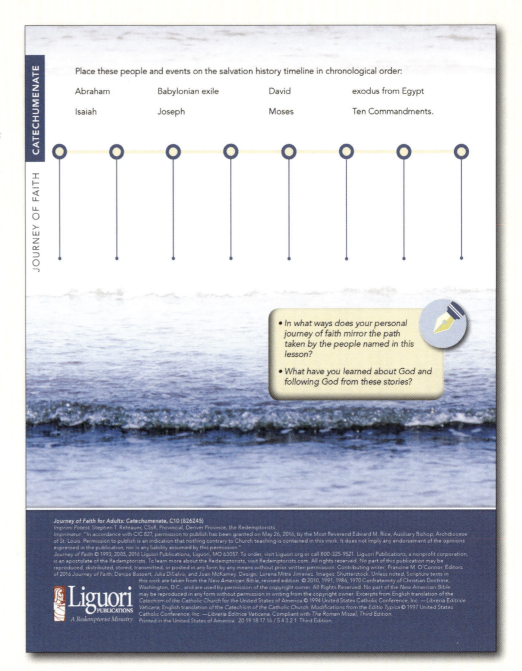

Journey of Faith for Adults, Catechumenate Leader Guide

Journaling

Have participants reflect on their faith journey. Encourage them to review the personal timelines and milestones they recorded for lesson C1. Guide them in responding to the lesson's prompts and the following questions: *How am I like Abraham in following the promptings of the Lord? When have I been like Joseph's brothers and seen God use my mistakes for his greater glory? What is my faith story and lineage?*

Closing Prayer

Have the participants and sponsors express any personal intentions, then pray together this excerpt from Exodus 15:

*I will sing to the LORD, for he is
  gloriously triumphant;
horse and chariot he has cast into
  the sea.
My strength and my refuge is
  the LORD,
and he has become my savior.
This is my God, I praise him;
the God of my father, I extol him....
your right hand, O LORD, shattered
  the enemy.
In your great majesty you
  overthrew your adversaries;...
In your love you led the people
  you redeemed;
in your strength you guided them
  to your holy dwelling.
The place you made the base
  of your throne, LORD,
the sanctuary, LORD, your hands
  established.
May the LORD reign forever
  and ever!*

Looking Ahead

Lesson C11: *The Early Church* continues the biblical narrative and participants' study of salvation history. It transitions from the establishment and protection of God's people in the Old Testament to the fulfillment of the covenant, salvation of the faithful, and establishment of the Christian Church in and through Jesus in the New Testament.

Invite the participants to review inquiry lesson Q4: *Who Is Jesus Christ?* and to pay special attention to the second readings (epistles) at Mass over the next few weeks. Encourage them to use the Lord's Prayer and Doxology as simple daily prayers.

The People of God

C11: The Early Church

Catechism: 731–76

Objectives

Participants will...

- identify the early Church as beginning at Pentecost.
- Understand the unique and respective calls of Sts. Peter and Paul to preach to the Jewish people and the Gentiles.
- recall major events and trends in Church history and practice during its first three centuries, including the martyrdom of St. Stephen, Roman persecution of Christians, and Constantine's Edict of Milan.

Leader Meditation

Matthew 10:5–42

Read and reflect on the mission of the apostles. How is their mission similar to your own as Christ's witness? When have you felt like a "sheep in the midst of wolves?" When have you felt comforted by Christ's words, "Even all the hairs of your head are counted. So do not be afraid?"

Related *Catholic Update*

- "Ten Peak Moments of Church History" (C8706A)

Leader Preparation

- Read the lesson, this lesson plan, the opening Scripture, and the *Catechism* sections.
- Be familiar with the following vocabulary terms: Pentecost, missionary. Definitions are provided in this guide's glossary.
- Gather copies of the Apostles' Creed for participants who don't have one.

Welcome

Greet each person as he or she arrives. Check for supplies and immediate needs. Solicit questions or comments about the previous session. Begin promptly.

Opening Scripture

Matthew 10:5–42

Light the candle and read the passage aloud. Point out especially Jesus' instructions that his disciples are to go "to the lost sheep"; to "proclaim the kingdom of God" (Luke 9:2); to "cure the sick"; and to give without payment. Ask participants to name ways in which the Church still carries out its mission.

> Before all else there is the choice of the twelve with Peter as their head. Representing the twelve tribes of Israel, they are the foundation stones of the new Jerusalem. The Twelve and the other disciples share in Christ's mission and his power, but also in his lot."
>
> CCC 765

Journey of Faith for Adults, Catechumenate Leader Guide

In Short:
- The coming of the Holy Spirit at Pentecost marks the Church's beginning.
- Followers of Christ quickly grew beyond a Jewish sect to include Gentiles.
- Persecution of Christians was common until Constantine decreed religious tolerance.

The Early Church

Catholics mark the descent of the Holy Spirit at Pentecost as the start of the Church. The Spirit has helped believers spread the message of Christ. The first followers of Jesus couldn't have envisioned today's Church, with more than a billion people and spanning the globe.

Did Jesus Start the Church?

It's clear from reading the New Testament that Jesus founded a Church and chose a group of twelve to follow him. He appointed Peter the leader of this Church:

> "Jesus said to him, ...'Blessed are you, Simon son of Jonah. For flesh and blood has not revealed this to you, but my heavenly Father. And so I say to you, you are Peter, and upon this rock I will build my church, and the gates of the netherworld shall not prevail against it.'"
>
> Matthew 16:17–18

Just as his new name indicated ("rock" in Aramaic and Greek), Peter became the foundation of Christ's Church.

The apostles were commissioned to carry the good news of Christ to the ends of the earth. They would speak in the name of Jesus. Responding to the circumstances of daily life and discerning the guidance of the Holy Spirit, they grew to understand the path on which God was leading them.

The Day the Church Was Born

The descent of the Holy Spirit on **Pentecost** is considered the birthday of the Church. After Jesus ascended to heaven, the Twelve feared for their lives and gathered in a locked room. As Jesus had directed, the apostles and Mary, Jesus' mother, prayed and waited for the Holy Spirit.

> "Suddenly there came from the sky a noise like a strong driving wind, and it filled the entire house in which they were. Then there appeared to them tongues of fire, which parted and came to rest on each one of them. And they were all filled with the holy Spirit and began to speak in different tongues, as the Spirit enabled them to proclaim."
>
> Acts 2:2–4

Although the apostles spoke in Aramaic, the foreign-born Jews celebrating the feast of Pentecost in Jerusalem understood them. Each person heard the apostles' words as if they were spoken in his or her own tongue.

CCC 731–76

The Early Church

Ask the participants to describe their own experiences with new beginnings. Emphasize that uncertainty is an important part of growth; growth almost always involves risking mistakes.

Did Jesus Start the Church?

Explain to catechumens the meaning and importance of the word *commissioned*: to be given a special purpose of mission. The apostles were commissioned by Jesus to spread the good news; in Christian baptism they will be (and candidates *are*) commissioned to do the same.

[Handwritten note: Matthew 10:8 ... without cost you have received, without cost you are to give.]

The Early Church

Christians or Jews?

Clarify that although the Jewish people aren't members of Christ's body or teach the fullness of truth, they still retain the covenant, promises, and revelation of the Old Testament (*CCC* 839–40). The Church honors them as ancestors in faith and continues to dialogue with Jewish leaders in the hope of achieving full unity.

Discuss rituals practiced in the early Church that remain important in the Church today—breaking bread, listening to the word, baptism following a period of instruction (the RCIA). You may also review the Jewish roots of the sacraments and other Catholic practices—referring to previous lessons if necessary—to deepen this continuity:

Examples include proclaiming Scripture in the synagogue (Luke 4:16–22), praying/reciting psalms (Ephesians 5:18–19; Colossians 3:16), and eucharistic roots in the Passover seder and other liturgical norms (Exodus 12; Leviticus 23; Deuteronomy 16; Matthew 5:17–20; CCC 1164, 2175).

Desire for Good News

Invite participants to share their response to the question, "What does Christianity offer that you haven't found anywhere else?" Ask them how they might incorporate these gifts or truths into their lives so that their personal witness might attract others to the Church.

On that day, Peter preached that the Messiah, predicted of old, had come and had been crucified. Many people came forward to be baptized.

Christians or Jews?

The early followers of Christ still followed their Jewish roots even though they believed in Jesus as the long-awaited Messiah. They looked forward to Christ's return and eternal reign.

The crucified Messiah was bound to become a stumbling block to the Jews. While Christ's followers prayed in the Temple as good Jews, they also met privately in homes for the "breaking of bread," the sacrifice the Savior had left them. This rite was a pledge of his return. The Eucharist was the bond that would hold them together until he returned.

This bond still holds us together as one.

- How did Jesus fulfill the hopes of the Jews who accepted him as their Messiah? How might he fulfill your hopes?

When Did Christians Separate From Judaism?

Judaism might have tolerated the followers of Christ had not Stephen, in preaching about Jesus, minimized the importance of the Temple. He emphasized the worship of God in spirit and in truth, not merely in the Temple. Stephen was stoned to death by a mob. Stephen's death for his faith made him the first Christian martyr. His final words are captured in sacred Scripture:

> "Lord Jesus, receive my spirit....Lord, do not hold this sin against them."
>
> Acts 7:59–60

Christianity Spreads

Persecution against the followers of Christ broke out in Jerusalem (see Acts 8:1). It forced most of Jesus' followers to leave the city. By the time the Romans destroyed the Temple in AD 70, Christianity had spread well beyond Jerusalem.

In Antioch, disciples realized they were no longer Jews awaiting the Messiah. The Messiah had come! His name is Jesus Christ. Therefore, they became known as "Christians" (see Acts 11:26).

When Peter received the Roman centurion, Cornelius, into the Church, the Holy Spirit showed the followers that salvation was for all people, not merely for Jews.

The zealous Pharisee named Saul opposed this growing community and their faith. He was determined to crush them. An encounter with the risen Christ converted Saul to Christianity (Acts 9:1–9).

Saul, now called Paul, became a great Christian **missionary**, taking the good news of Christ to others. He preached first to the Jews, but when they rejected him he went to the Gentiles, that is, people who were not Jews. Paul ran into many conflicts, some from Jews who regarded him as a traitor, some from those who made their living from idol worship, but he also gained many converts.

- Who helped bring the good news of Jesus to you?

Desire for Good News

Christianity spread quickly. God used many factors to open hearts to the gift of salvation.

Public morality in the Roman Empire was very low. Divorce destroyed upper-class family life. To keep people entertained, the emperors and officials

---

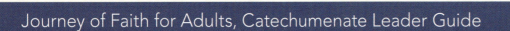

Journey of Faith for Adults, Catechumenate Leader Guide

sponsored public spectacles that appealed to blood lust or immorality. The public cult of the mythological gods, encouraged by the government to maintain order, didn't foster morality or offer hope in the face of death. Many religions of Egypt and Persia led people further away from God.

Reaction against immorality and brutality—as well as a concern for salvation after death—caused many people to welcome the good news of Christ. Rome was tolerant of different religious beliefs, which meant Christians managed to live in peace. In spite of later persecutions, there were several million believers by the year 300.

- What does Christianity offer that you haven't found anywhere else?

Why Were Christians Persecuted?

When Rome burned in the year 64, Nero blamed the Christians for the fire. He had Christians crucified and ignited as human torches. It was during Nero's persecution that both Peter and Paul died as martyrs for Christ.

The Christians were an easy scapegoat. Nero blamed them for everything that went wrong and decreed that no one could profess Christianity. Romans accused Christians of crimes and terrible behaviors—from treason (because Christians refused to worship the emperor) to cannibalism (because Romans misunderstood the Eucharist).

By the third century, the growing number of Christians made it clear that persecution was failing. Every time a Christian died for the faith, others realized there was something unusual and special about this group, leading to more people being baptized. In a dynamic the oppressors didn't anticipate, persecution led to the growth of Christianity.

- When have you experienced persecution?

Challenges From Within

The early Church also had to contend with internal strife. Many Christians denied their faith to save their lives in times of persecution only to return to the Church when persecutions subsided. Christian communities were divided about what to do with those who wished to return after denying their faith. They decided to accept them back after a period of public penance.

Life in the Early Church

Despite persecution and doctrinal wrangling, the Church developed and grew. After lengthy instruction, new members were baptized, usually by immersion in a river. The ceremony of the breaking of bread, the Eucharist or Mass, bound the Christian community together in the real flesh and blood of Jesus.

When baptized Christians sinned and sought forgiveness, they were forgiven and given a penance to indicate their contrition and firm resolve to follow Christ anew.

Bishops, as successors of the apostles, shepherded the Church in their particular areas. In larger communities, the bishop would ordain presbyters (priests) to assist him. Deacons saw to the various charities of the Church, instructed the faithful, and distributed the Eucharist.

Each bishop who succeeded Peter as bishop of Rome (the pope) was seen as having authority in the wider Church. As early as the year 97, Pope Clement in Rome exercised power over a dispute in Corinth.

Saint Irenaeus (130–200) said in his book *Against Heresies* that if a local bishop taught the same thing as the bishop of Rome, he was surely teaching the faith of Christ: "For with this Church [Rome], because of its superior origin, all churches must agree, that is, all the faithful in the whole world. And it is in her that the faithful everywhere have maintained the apostolic tradition" (*Against Heresies*, 3:3:2).

CATECHUMENATE · JOURNEY OF FAITH

Why Were Christians Persecuted?

Ask participants if they have ever felt (or currently feel) like a sheep among wolves. Invite them to share and record their responses to this and the lesson's question, "When have you experienced persecution?" in their journals. If a participant is struggling with real or perceived persecution from close family, friends, or the Church itself, privately offer some personal or pastoral support.

Discuss why Christians will sometimes come into conflict with or oppose the secular, political, dominant, or popular culture. Remind catechumens that the words, actions, and life of Jesus also created scandal and upset the religious and political leaders of his time. The Church follows the truth of Christ, proclaiming it to be the way to achieve the common good, bring others to salvation and unity, and fulfill the dignity and purpose of the human person. Not all will believe, understand, or practice our ways, but we believe full knowledge (revelation) and manifestation of God's kingdom are yet to come.

Life in the Early Church

Compare the faith journey of the early Church with the personal faith journeys of those present. Assure participants that most Christians go through periods of uncertainty, trial, and tremendous growth. Offer examples from the saints if there's time.

The Early Church

Constantine and Christianity

In 303, Diocletian unleashed the worst persecution against Christians yet. It resulted in the deaths of thousands of Christians in Asia Minor, Africa, and Greece. This persecution lasted through his two successors. In 312, at the battle of Milvian Bridge, the western Emperor Constantine had a dream in which Christ told him to use the sign of the cross against his enemies. Constantine marked his soldiers' shields with the cross.

Constantine won the battle and gave credit to the God of the Christians for his success. In 313, Constantine decreed that no one "should be denied the opportunity to give his heart to the observance of the Christian religion" (Edict of Milan). Christians could finally live and proclaim their faith openly.

- *What might the world be like today without the presence and influence of Christianity?*
- *Some say we stand on the shoulders of those who came before us. What does that mean to you in relation to what you've learned about the history of the Church?*

Journey of Faith for Adults: Catechumenate, C11 (826245)
Imprimi Potest: Stephen T. Rehrauer, CSsR, Provincial, Denver Province, the Redemptorists.
Imprimatur: "In accordance with CIC 827, permission to publish has been granted on May 26, 2016, by the Most Reverend Edward M. Rice, Auxiliary Bishop, Archdiocese of St. Louis. Permission to publish is an indication that nothing contrary to Church teaching is contained in this work. It does not imply any endorsement of the opinions expressed in the publication, nor is any liability assumed by this permission."
Journey of Faith © 1993, 2005, 2016 Liguori Publications, Liguori, MO 63057. To order, visit Liguori.org or call 800-325-9521. Liguori Publications, a nonprofit corporation, is an apostolate of the Redemptorists. To learn more about the Redemptorists, visit Redemptorists.com. All rights reserved. No part of this publication may be reproduced, distributed, stored, transmitted, or posted in any form by any means without prior written permission. Contributing writers: Edward Day, CSsR, and Richard A. Boever, CSsR. Editors of 2016 Journey of Faith: Denise Bossert, Julia DiSalvo, and Joan McKamey. Design: Lorena Mitre Jimenez. Images: Shutterstock. Unless noted, Scripture texts in this work are taken from the *New American Bible*, revised edition: © 2010, 1991, 1986, 1970 Confraternity of Christian Doctrine, Washington, D.C., and are used by permission of the copyright owner. All Rights Reserved. No part of the *New American Bible* may be reproduced in any form without permission in writing from the copyright owner. Excerpts from English translation of the *Catechism of the Catholic Church for the United States of America* © 1994 United States Catholic Conference, Inc.—Libreria Editrice Vaticana; English translation of the *Catechism of the Catholic Church: Modifications from the Editio Typica* © 1997 United States Catholic Conference, Inc.—Libreria Editrice Vaticana. Compliant with *The Roman Missal, Third Edition*.
Printed in the United States of America. 20 19 18 17 16 / 5 4 3 2 1. Third Edition.

LIGUORI PUBLICATIONS
A Redemptorist Ministry

Journey of Faith for Adults, Catechumenate Leader Guide

Journaling

Explain that the gift of faith is a blessing and a responsibility. Encourage participants to reflect more on their life stories and to share in their journals why they feel God is calling them to the Church. Ask them, "What helps you to remain faithful to the calling? What might be the next chapter in your story of sainthood?"

Closing Prayer

After acknowledging any special intentions, recite the Apostles' Creed as a group. If you have only one copy, you may wish to pass it around the group, allowing each participant to read a few lines before passing it to the next person.

Looking Ahead

Lesson C12: *Church History* continues the overview of the Church in time with Constantine and into the twenty-first century. Encourage participants, especially Protestant candidates, to prepare specific questions about major Church events such as the Crusades, the Reformation, and Vatican II. While all might not be answered to their satisfaction, it will certainly bring concerns or misunderstandings to light and direct the leaders to where additional formation or information is needed.

Invite them to review inquiry lessons Q6: *Divine Revelation* and Q13: *The Church as Community*, which discuss the nature of the Church and Church teachings beyond, yet founded and united in, the institutional hierarchy.

The Early Church

C12: Church History

Catechism: 811–70

Objectives

Participants will…

- identify major events and trends—both positive and negative—in Church history from the Edict of Milan in 313 to Vatican II in the 1960s and beyond.
- recall several figures, saints, and religious institutes that helped to shape and guide the Church throughout history.
- recognize that the Holy Spirit guides and protects the Church from both external and internal troubles.

Leader Meditation

Matthew 28:16–20

Jesus breathed life into his Church, and these words still hold the Church together and give it life today: "I am with you always, until the end of the age." Quiet yourself and hear Jesus saying these words to you. Talk to him as you would a friend, your Savior, your Creator, the eucharistic Lord who comes to you so intimately at Mass—because he is all these things. Contemplate the reality that God has been present to and in his people throughout history. The Lord, who leads the Church, promises to be with each one of us every day. Determine some ways to share that amazing truth with each RCIA participant and implement them.

Related *Catholic Update*

- "Ten Achievements of Vatican II" (C1301A)

Leader Preparation

- Read the lesson, this lesson plan, the opening Scripture, and the *Catechism* sections.
- Be familiar with the following vocabulary terms: heresy, schism, denomination. Definitions are provided in this guide's glossary.
- Gather some basic materials or references on Church history to distribute (or loan out) to participants. Audio and/or visual aids such as timelines, charts, artwork, and news items will help build context and make these events and figures come to life.

Welcome

Greet each person as he or she arrives. Check for supplies and immediate needs. Solicit questions or comments about the previous session. Begin promptly.

Opening Scripture

Matthew 28:16–20

Light the candle and read the passage aloud. Point out the many aspects of this scene that are still present in the Church today: worshiping and doubtful disciples, the call to baptize and obey the commandments, God's assistance, and the need to evangelize others. Ask the participants, "Was this message intended only for the apostles, or is it also directed to all of us here today?"

> The Church is catholic because Christ is present in her.…The Church was, in this fundamental sense, catholic on the day of Pentecost and will always be so until the day of the Parousia.
>
> *CCC 830*

Journey of Faith for Adults, Catechumenate Leader Guide

Journey of Faith

C12 CATECHUMENATE

Point out that even in the early Church, religious freedom encompassed more than public worship and included private devotion, moral living, and social action. When the Church today defends religious freedom, it is trying to protect our ability to live according to the truth and to proclaim it to others.

In Short:
- The Church has a rich and varied history.
- Saints and religious orders helped shape the Church.
- The Spirit guides the Church.

Church History

Your life story reflects the events and experiences that make you who you are. Getting to know you involves learning about significant moments in your history. It's the same with the Catholic Church. Like our own personal stories, the story of the Church is a journey of faith.

- Think of an event from your journey that affects who you are today.

Religious Freedom

In 313, Constantine decreed that no one "should be denied the opportunity to give his heart to the observance of the Christian religion" (Edict of Milan). Christians could finally live and proclaim their faith openly.

Freed from concern about persecution, Christians had time to think about the truths of God's revelation through Jesus Christ. Many great thinkers explored the Church's understanding of God. This period also produced some whose thoughts wandered far from the course set by Jesus during his earthly ministry.

Heresies, beliefs or opinions that directly contradict official Church teaching, emerged. One heresy said Jesus wasn't divine, and another said Jesus wasn't human. Some emperors supported heresies and executed Christians for disagreeing with them.

Even with these challenges, incidents of martyrdom (dying for the faith) declined as Christianity became more accepted in the Roman Empire. Christians found new ways to dedicate their lives to Jesus. Some chose to go to the desert to focus on penance and prayer. These men and women felt the solitary life kept them away from society's corruption. Religious communities formed as people began to gather around these holy men and women. Other Christians put their faith into action through social service. They provided compassionate care to the poor, sick, dying, and abandoned.

- What might the hermits have found in the desert that's more difficult to find in ordinary life?
- How can you create a desert space in your spiritual life?

ADULTS

CCC 811–870

Church History

Invite participants to share their responses to the opening prompt (a life event that affected their faith journey or who they are today). Emphasize that the Church, too, has a long history; the Church is not stagnant but ever changing, ever growing. Clarify that this doesn't mean God or the truth ever changes; the Church simply discovers new revelations within and applications of Christian principles and values to our changing world.

Religious Freedom

Clarify the difference between *heresy* and ignorance. Explain that some may not agree with Church teachings because they don't fully understand them or are led astray by false teachers. Others may simply struggle to accept them because they need more faith. A true heretic rejects the truth and closes himself or herself off to God's word. If it helps, read this quote from the *Catechism* aloud: "The ruptures that wound the unity of Christ's body—here we must distinguish heresy, apostasy, and schism—do not occur without human sin" (*CCC* 817).

Church History

Conquest, Collapse, and Confusion

In their journals, have participants reflect on any serious doubts about God, the Church, or Christian moral living they may have experienced or are currently experiencing. Chances are, these issues have appeared elsewhere in Church history and have been responded to. Encourage them to seek out the answers in Scripture, the magisterium, their sponsor, and other trusted sources.

Emphasize that because the Church comprises human beings, there have been Church leaders and thinkers who have wandered from the course set by Jesus. Our hope lies not in individuals or institutions alone but in the Holy Spirit, who works through instruments and charisms to keep us on course and in God's grace.

Conquest, Collapse, and Confusion

In the fifth century, the Roman Empire began to collapse as barbarian tribes invaded. Bishops became the only authorities people could rely on, not only for Church teaching but also for maintaining social order. Initially, Roman Christians wanted nothing to do with the barbarian conquerors. Eventually, Christians worked to civilize and convert these invaders.

As missionaries, these men and women worked to bring the faith to unbelievers, often through social service. Monasteries and parishes were founded to bring the newly converted to a deeper knowledge of Christianity. The educated monks helped instruct the people while parishes made Christianity the center of community life. Service to the poor was almost completely up to the Church. The invaders employed the clergy (ordained Church officials) as ambassadors and public leaders.

Serious problems arose as a result of the close ties between Church and state. Nobles chose who would become bishops, often selecting men who would support their interests rather than the gospel. Priests were appointed by local landowners and often had little or no training. Many clergy and religious became more interested in material possessions and power than in spreading the good news.

- To whom do you turn for clarity and truth in times of confusion? How might that person or organization be a vehicle of God's wisdom for you?

Back to Basics

The eleventh and twelfth centuries saw the flowering of great universities, Gothic architecture, and extraordinary thinkers and scholars. These centuries also brought new problems to the Church. In 1054, disagreement about the pope's role and a difference in understanding of how we talk about the Holy Spirit in the Creed led to a **schism** or division of the Eastern (Orthodox) Church from Rome.

Saint Bernard (1090–1153) and others brought reform to religious communities, asking them to return to a life of prayer. Their reform spread throughout the rest of the Church. Finally, Pope Gregory VII took back the power to appoint clergy from the nobles.

In addition to the noble desire to protect Christianity's holy sites, baser motives—greed and a desire for power—fueled the Crusades (1095–1291). In a series of military expeditions, Christians of Western Europe attempted to take Jerusalem and the Holy Land from the Muslims.

While the Crusades continued through most of the thirteenth century, the Church of this time also had people of remarkable character. Saints Francis of Assisi and Dominic changed the way Christianity was preached. Monasteries preserved the teachings of the Church but had lost contact with the common people who needed this knowledge. Francis, Dominic, and their followers took the gospel message to the streets and lived simply among the people. Saint Thomas Aquinas, a Dominican priest, was an important philosopher and theologian of this time.

- Reform often leads to renewal. When have you experienced new life, energy, or clarity of purpose as a result of changing your ways?

Back to Basics

Refer or direct participants to additional materials or resources for details regarding the Great Schism, Crusades, Inquisition, Protestant Reformation, or other events (see activity, below). Avoid confusing or misleading participants with speculation or commentary. Stick to the basic facts and authoritative sources.

Journey of Faith for Adults, Catechumenate Leader Guide

The Call for Reform

The fourteenth and fifteenth centuries were fraught with confusion. At times, two and three men claimed to be pope. Corruption among many Church leaders and interference in the Church by secular authorities increased. Saint Catherine of Siena and others called for renewal.

In 1517, Martin Luther, a Catholic monk, called for an end to the abuses in the Church. He wanted reform, not a new Church. Yet poor communication, stubbornness on both sides, and interference by secular authorities led him to take a "protestant" position and break away from Catholicism. Division followed division, and Christianity has since split into thousands of **denominations**.

This Protestant Reformation shocked Catholic leadership into action. The Council of Trent (1545–1563) clarified Catholic belief, corrected abuses, and set up the seminary system to educate clergy. New religious orders began to help in renewal and promotion of spiritual growth.

- How does an emphasis on social service show the Church's roots in Jesus' ministry?

The Call to Serve

Social service and everyday spirituality were the focus of the seventeenth and eighteenth centuries. Saint Francis de Sales wrote books that called laypeople (those not ordained) to holiness. Saints Vincent de Paul and Louise de Marillac organized ways to help the poor. They set up groups of laypeople, called "confraternities," to manage orphanages, homes for the elderly, and parish services for the needy.

Catholicism in America

In the early 1800s, Catholics were a small and insignificant number in the United States. By the Civil War, they had become the largest single religious group in the United States, numbering three and a half million people.

This increase in numbers was the result of large numbers of immigrants coming from Ireland and Germany. Later, many Catholics from Poland, Italy, Mexico, Canada, and Eastern European countries came to America. Catholic immigrants were often subject to discrimination and misunderstanding.

Modern Catholic Social Teaching began as the result of the Industrial Revolution. In 1891, Pope Leo XIII spoke out in support of the rights of working people. He believed in the workers' rights to fair wages and safe working conditions, forming unions and striking if needed.

The Twentieth-century Church

The Second Vatican Council (1962–65) took a close look at the Church and its relationship to the modern world. The council made updates in the ways Catholics worship and practice their faith. Calling the Church the "people of God" and teaching of the "universal call to holiness," it encouraged the laity to become more involved in the work of the Church and to renew their efforts to follow Christ.

> "The laity 'work for the sanctification of the world from within as a leaven. In this way they may make Christ known to others, especially by the testimony of a life resplendent in faith, hope and charity.'"
>
> *Dogmatic Constitution on the Church (Lumen Gentium)*, 31

Many Catholic Christians give their lives selflessly to advance the causes of peace and justice. Dorothy Day, cofounder of the Catholic Worker movement, and St. Teresa of Calcutta, founder of the Missionaries of Charity in India, worked heroically to make God's love real to the poor.

During his time as pope (1978–2005), St. John Paul II asked forgiveness for sins committed in the name of the Catholic Church through the ages. Some of the wrongdoings he listed were the censure of Galileo, involvement in the slave trade, injustices against women, inactivity and silence during the Holocaust, and cases of clergy sex abuse.

The Call for Reform

Invite candidates to share how their perspective of the Catholic Church has changed since entering the RCIA process. Ask them, "What beliefs or preconceived notions have been enlightened by the truth? What challenges have been overcome or remain?" Affirm their ongoing work of conversion.

Catholicism in America

Emphasize the importance and challenges of having a *universal* Church. Each culture, language, rite, nation, tribe, and generation offers a unique gift to the Church and to the world, yet also has unique spiritual needs. As globalization and diversity increase, we remain united in our one, eternal God.

Point out that Catholic social teaching will be discussed in detail in lesson C16: *Social Justice*.

The Twentieth-century Church

Discuss the important changes in Church thinking that resulted from the Second Vatican Council, such as the role of laypeople, reforms to make the liturgy more meaningful to people in their own language and culture, and the importance of social justice. Refer or direct participants to additional materials or resources as needed (see activity on the next page).

Church History

The Church Today...and Beyond

Ask participants to list some challenges facing the Catholic Church and many other Christian churches today.

Responses may include, but are not limited to, materialism; decreases in Church membership and religious behaviors; medical and technological advances that threaten human life and dignity; and opposition to Catholic teachings on marriage, sexuality, and family or the relationship between Church and state/society.

Assist participants in researching Church history further by suggesting some reliable resources to begin with. Encourage sponsors to join their catechumen or candidate in this work; it is an opportunity to learn more and to strengthen their relationship.

JOURNEY OF FAITH   CATECHUMENATE

The Church Today...and Beyond

Today's Church takes a strong stand on moral and social issues, such as abortion, assisted suicide, and religious liberty. It remains active in aiding the poor and oppressed of the world.

In every age, the Church experiences both opportunities and challenges and produces both saints and scoundrels. As it faces new challenges and learns from past errors, the Church remains the living sacrament of the body of Christ in our world. We trust the Holy Spirit to guide the Church as it follows Jesus' command:

"Go, therefore, and make disciples of all nations, baptizing them in the name of the Father, and of the Son, and of the holy Spirit, teaching them to observe all that I have commanded you."

Matthew 28:19–20

Choose an event in Church history that you'd like to learn more about. Do some research and consider the following questions:

- *What value was the Church trying to uphold?*
- *What effect did human goodness and/or weakness have on this event?*
- *How do you see the Spirit at work guiding the Church through this event?*

Spend some time in prayer, reflecting on the following question. Be sure to open your heart for God's response—within your prayer time and in the days ahead. Record your reflection in your journal.

- *The future of the Catholic Church depends on the Holy Spirit and your response to what God calls you to do. What role might God want you to play in the unfolding life of the Church?*

Journey of Faith for Adults: Catechumenate, C12 (826245)
Imprimi Potest: Stephen T. Rehrauer, CSsR, Provincial, Denver Province, the Redemptorists.
Imprimatur: "In accordance with CIC 827, permission to publish has been granted on May 26, 2016, by the Most Reverend Edward M. Rice, Auxiliary Bishop, Archdiocese of St. Louis. Permission to publish is an indication that nothing contrary to Church teaching is contained in this work. It does not imply any endorsement of the opinions expressed in the publication; nor is any liability assumed by this permission."
Journey of Faith © 1993, 2005, 2016 Liguori Publications, Liguori, MO 63057. To order, visit Liguori.org or call 800-325-9521. Liguori Publications, a nonprofit corporation, is an apostolate of the Redemptorists. To learn more about the Redemptorists, visit Redemptorists.com. All rights reserved. No part of this publication may be reproduced, distributed, stored, transmitted, or posted in any form by any means without prior written permission. Contributing writers: Fr. Oscar Lukefahr, CM; Edward Day, CSsR, and Richard A. Boever, CSsR. Editors of 2016 Journey of Faith: Denise Bossert, Julia DiSalvo, and Joan McKamey. Design: Lorena Mitre Jimenez. Images: Shutterstock. Unless noted, Scripture texts in this work are taken from the New American Bible, revised edition © 2010, 1991, 1986, 1970 Confraternity of Christian Doctrine, Washington, D.C., and are used by permission of the copyright owner. All Rights Reserved. No part of the New American Bible may be reproduced in any form without permission in writing from the copyright owner. Excerpts from English translation of the Catechism of the Catholic Church for the United States of America © 1994 United States Catholic Conference, Inc. —Libreria Editrice Vaticana; English translation of the Catechism of the Catholic Church: Modifications from the Editio Typica © 1997 United States Catholic Conference, Inc. —Libreria Editrice Vaticana. Excerpts from Vatican documents © 2016 Libreria Editrice Vaticana and are used with permission. Compliant with The Roman Missal, Third Edition.
Printed in the United States of America. 20 19 18 17 16 / 5 4 3 2 1. Third Edition.

Liguori PUBLICATIONS
A Redemptorist Ministry

Journey of Faith for Adults, Catechumenate Leader Guide

Journaling

Remind participants to listen to God as much as they speak and write this week—perhaps even more. However, recording their thoughts on their role in the life of the Church will encourage them to pursue their vocations and ministries after the Easter Vigil.

Closing Prayer

After asking for special intentions, pray the Lord's Prayer together, keeping in mind that this prayer has been with the Church throughout its history.

Take-home

Remind participants to complete the activity and journaling exercises this week. As they explore and reflect, have them consider how the Church is uniquely empowered to share the gospel message, to make disciples, and to speak on matters of morality and social justice. This mission is universal and timeless.

C12

Church History

C13: Christian Moral Living

Catechism: 1730–1802, 1950–86

Objectives

Participants will…

- recognize that the moral law comes from God.
- realize that human freedom (free will) does not imply moral autonomy.
- accept that we are called to form our consciences according to Christ's teachings, Scripture, the Church, and the writings of saints and theologians.
- realize that the ultimate goal is to love as Christ loves, not merely to avoid sinning.

Leader Meditation

Proverbs 3:1–12

Reflect silently on this passage, which directs us to "trust in the Lord," to rely on his intelligence alone, to remain "mindful of him," and not to spurn his discipline. Consider those times when you have turned to the Church (or failed to) for discernment. Ask yourself, "When has it been hard to follow the Church's teaching? Have I found sufficient peace and grace when I followed Christ's way, even when it was difficult?"

Related *Catholic Updates*

- "The Ten Commandments: Sounds of Love From Sinai" (C8909A)
- "Understanding Sin Today" (C9701A)
- "Catholic Morality: Has It Changed?" (C9608A)
- "Your Conscience and Church Teaching: How Do They Fit Together?" (C8212A)

Leader Preparation

- Read the lesson, this lesson plan, the opening Scripture, and the *Catechism* sections.
- Be familiar with the term conscience and how it relates to freedom, responsibility, and morality. Its definition can be found in this guide's glossary.
- Purchase a recording of "Restless" by Audrey Assad and Matt Maher to play during the Closing Prayer (from *The House You're Building*, © 2010 Sparrow).

Welcome

Greet each person as he or she arrives. Solicit questions or comments about the previous session(s) and begin promptly.

Opening Scripture

Proverbs 3:1–12

Light the candle and read the passage aloud. Point out that many fall into the trap of leaning on their own understanding of right and wrong. They may deny God's presence or authority or the existence of any universal morality: *It's true (right) for me.* Others sincerely attempt to follow a path claiming to be moral or even Christian, but all of these cannot be truly and fully correct. Admit that even faithful Catholics sometimes rush or avoid decisions or fail to offer the Lord a say in their daily choices. Encourage participants to turn to the Church for wisdom rather than to definitions of good and bad that are constantly changing.

> Freedom makes man a moral subject….Human acts, that is, acts that are freely chosen in consequence of a judgment of conscience, can be morally evaluated. They are either good or evil.
> *CCC 1749*

Journey of Faith for Adults, Catechumenate Leader Guide

Journey of Faith

C13 — CATECHUMENATE

In Short:

- Morality is ordered by God, who gives us free will to choose right or wrong.
- Jesus' teachings, the Bible, and the Church help us form good consciences.
- God calls us to reflect on our choices and behaviors in the light of love.

Christian Moral Living

Jesus promised, "Whoever loves me will keep my word, and my Father will love him, and we will come to him and make our dwelling with him" (John 14:23). We accept Jesus Christ as our guide, believing that his words and example teach us the best way to live. We try to apply his teachings to the decisions of daily life. But God gives us free will, the freedom to receive or reject his love, to choose to do right or wrong.

> "Jesus said, 'Not everyone who says to me, "Lord, Lord," will enter the kingdom of heaven, but only the one who does the will of my Father in heaven.'"
>
> Matthew 7:21

- How can we know God's will? How do we know what choices to make?

Following Your Conscience

Conscience is our sense of the moral goodness or evil of a thing. Our conscience helps us to discern right from wrong and to accept the responsibility to choose what's right.

Saint Paul wrote that our basic notions of right and wrong come from God:

> "The demands of the law are written in their hearts, while their conscience also bears witness."
>
> Romans 2:15

> "For man has in his heart a law written by God; to obey it is the very dignity of man; according to it he will be judged. Conscience is the most secret core and sanctuary of a man. There he is alone with God, Whose voice echoes in his depths. In a wonderful manner conscience reveals that law which is fulfilled by love of God and neighbor."
>
> Pastoral Constitution on the Church in the Modern World (Gaudium et Spes), 16

> "The perfection of the moral good consists in man's being moved to the good not only by his will but also by his 'heart.'"
>
> CCC 1775

ADULTS

CCC 1730–1802, 1950–86

Christian Moral Living

Ask participants how they make decisions, especially major or difficult ones. Ask, "Do you have a general process, and if so, what steps do you take?" Emphasize the importance of gathering facts, weighing pros and cons (costs and benefits), determining priorities, and considering the consequences to self and others. Review the "STOP Method" box in the lesson on page three and encourage them to practice it. Point out that lesson M4: *Discernment* also provides tips and steps for making responsible, Christian, moral decisions.

Following Your Conscience

Discuss the true nature of freedom and responsibility. Clarify that having free will and a conscience "does not imply a right to say or do everything" (*CCC* 1740). Rather, our freedom allows us to choose the good, reject sin, and submit to his ways. In other words, God doesn't force faith or obedience; he wants willing disciples, not slaves. Read this *Catechism* quote aloud: "The more one does what is good, the freer one becomes. There is no true freedom except in the service of what is good and just" (*CCC* 1733; see also 1742).

Christian Moral Living

Forming Your Conscience

Point out that the ancient Jews had the Law of Moses, the commandments, and religious leaders to help them make good moral choices. The early Church also used these and other tools for moral guidance, such as when the Corinthians wrote to Paul for advice (1 Corinthians 7:1). Emphasize that, like them, Catholics can turn to the Bible, the teachings of Jesus and the Church, and family and friends when faced with a challenging decision.

The Law of Love Replaces Legalism

Remind participants that the Church's moral message can be summed up in the Golden Rule. Emphasize that Jesus takes the Ten Commandments a step further when he gives the two Great Commandments based on love rather than the Law (see also *CCC* 1789, 1972).

Proclaim Matthew 5:1–12, 17–20, then ask participants whether living the Beatitudes seems more difficult than obeying the Ten Commandments. Emphasize that Jesus challenges all his disciples to develop a strong moral character but also offers them the strength to persevere and to seek and offer forgiveness.

CATECHUMENATE — JOURNEY OF FAITH

Important choices shouldn't be subjective or emotional decisions. The teachings of Jesus Christ, the Bible, and the guidance of the Church help us form a good conscience.

- What laws are written in your heart?

Jesus Echoes the Old Testament

Our source for the study of Christ's teachings is the Bible, and our starting point is love:

"You shall love the Lord, your God, with all your heart, with all your soul, and with all your mind. This is the greatest and the first commandment. The second is like it: You shall love your neighbor as yourself."

Matthew 22:37–39

Jesus was echoing the Old Testament: the greatest and first commandment is from Deuteronomy (6:4–5) and the second from Leviticus (19:18).

When Jesus was asked, "What must I do to inherit eternal life?" [Jesus replied], "You know the commandments: 'You shall not kill; you shall not commit adultery; you shall not steal; you shall not bear false witness; you shall not defraud; honor your father and your mother'" (Mark 10:17, 19).

The Jews accepted the Ten Commandments as God's will. While escaping from slavery in Egypt, God gave the Israelites the commandments to keep them from falling into slavery to sin. These standards of morality have stood the test of time.

Find the Ten Commandments in the Old Testament (Exodus 20:1–20, Deuteronomy 5:1–21) and reflect on the question below.

- How would our world be different if everyone obeyed the Ten Commandments?

The Law of Love Replaces Legalism

Jesus did more than affirm the Ten Commandments. He gave us a higher standard: "You have heard that it was said to your ancestors, 'You shall not kill; and whoever kills will be liable to judgment.' But I say to you, whoever is angry with his brother will be liable to judgment" (Matthew 5:21–22). He said we must avoid lustful thoughts, not just adultery, and abandon old patterns that allowed divorce, revenge, and hatred in favor of love.

The Pharisees imposed strict requirements through their legal interpretations, based on their reading of the Hebrew Scriptures (Old Testament). When Jesus' disciples were hungry and began to pick heads of grain, the Pharisees accused them of harvesting, an activity forbidden on the Sabbath (Exodus 34:21). Jesus defended his followers, claiming the Sabbath was made for people and not people for the Sabbath (Mark 2:23–28). Love and life trump legalism.

In another example that scandalized the Pharisees, the Old Testament designated some food as unclean—not to be eaten, but Jesus challenged that. He explained that what we eat cannot make us unclean, but thoughts, words, and deeds that come from our hearts can (Mark 7:18–23).

In his teaching, Jesus urged us to move beyond legalism to what truly brings love. He said, "Do not think that I have come to abolish the law or the prophets. I have come not to abolish but to fulfill" (Matthew 5:17). Laws are necessary and good, but Christ's followers must view them according to Christ's mind and heart.

"Jesus said, 'Everyone who listens to these words of mine and acts on them will be like a wise man who built his house on rock. The rain fell, the floods came, and the winds blew and buffeted the house. But it did not collapse; it had been solidly set on rock.'"

Matthew 7:24–25

- How can you build your life on the rock of Jesus' words?

Journey of Faith for Adults, Catechumenate Leader Guide

The Church Guides Us

The teachings of the Church also help us form our consciences. Jesus is present in his Church and has given its leaders the authority to speak and act in his name.

Jesus told his disciples to go to all nations, "teaching them to observe all that I have commanded you" (Matthew 28:20). After his ascension, the apostles applied the commands of Jesus to the situations they encountered. The New Testament letters to early Christian communities offer moral guidance, and some give rules of conduct in matters of Church organization, relationships, and daily life.

The Church provides moral leadership through laws and instruction from pastors, bishops, and popes. While it's true that we are collectively the Church, each of us doesn't have the same authority or perform the same function. Saint Paul makes it clear that some members have the duty to guide us:

"And he gave some as apostles, others as prophets, others as evangelists, others as pastors and teachers, to equip the holy ones for the work of ministry, for building up the body of Christ."

Ephesians 4:11–12

Today, people face moral problems previous generations couldn't have imagined. Church leaders help us to apply the gospel to modern life. The Church provides moral leadership in many forms and in sometimes complex ways. But beautifully simple principles underlie them all: Avoid evil and pursue good. Follow the Golden Rule: treat others as you would like to be treated. Respect your fellow humans and their consciences (see CCC 1789).

"Trust in the LORD with all your heart, on your own intelligence do not rely; In all your ways be mindful of him, and he will make straight your paths."

Proverbs 3:5–6

- How open are you to seeking and following the guidance of the Catholic Church in matters of morality?

Teachers Inspire Us

Throughout Church history, there have been great teachers of moral theology and the spiritual life. They have helped form the consciences of generations of Catholics.

Some theologians and spiritual writers are qualified to offer moral guidance by reason of their education, experience, and adherence to Church teaching. The common practice of good Catholics, who are led by the Holy Spirit, can also guide us.

- Think of Catholics who have influenced you. What guides them?

STOP Method for Forming and Informing Your Conscience

Search out facts (consult Church teaching, scientific information, Bible, teachings of Jesus, instruction of moral theologians) by asking what, why, who, where, when, and how.

Think about alternatives to your proposed action and consider consequences.

Others should be consulted (faithful Catholics who've dealt with this question, others affected or involved), and the effect on others should be considered.

Pray for guidance.

Living Like Christ

It's possible to mistakenly assume that our goal in life is to avoid sin, but our real goal is to become more like Jesus, to act out of love rather than out of a sense of obligation.

The love of Christ challenges us to work for peace and social justice and to have concern for the poor. Christ cautioned us that our eternal destiny will be determined by our readiness to help others and reminded us that whatever we do for others is done for him (see Matthew 25:31–46).

The Church Guides Us

Review the difference between venial and mortal sin (lesson C6). Share this analogy: While breaking some laws results in a simple warning or small fine, others may lead to a revocation of rights, such as a license, or incarceration. Like crimes, certain sins have more severe consequences to self and others because the act is more serious (harmful).

Remind participants of the source of the Church's authority: "Whatever you bind on earth," Jesus said to Peter, "will be bound in heaven and whatever you loose on earth will be loosed in heaven" (Matthew 16:19). Clarify that while we may dislike or choose to disagree with certain words or actions of the pope and other Church leaders, dissent from the teaching authority of the Church—infallible doctrine (dogma) and the magisterium—is not accepted. Distinguish between authoritative teachings and pastoral responses. Emphasize the need to form one's conscience, to base one's judgments on accurate and reliable sources, and to humble oneself before the Lord.

The following quotes may help:

- "In matters of faith and morals, the bishops speak in the name of Christ and the faithful are to accept their teaching and adhere to it with a religious assent. This religious submission of mind and will must be shown in a special way to the authentic magisterium of the Roman Pontiff…" (Dogmatic Constitution on the Church, *Lumen Gentium*, 25).

- "A religious submission of the intellect and will must be given to a doctrine which the Supreme Pontiff or the college of bishops declares concerning faith or morals when they exercise the authentic magisterium, even if they do not intend to proclaim it by definitive act; therefore, the Christian faithful are to take care to avoid those things which do not agree with it" (Canon 752).

- "Christ, when He communicated His divine power to Peter and the other Apostles and sent them to teach all nations His commandments, constituted them as the authentic guardians and interpreters of the whole moral law, not only, that is, of the law of the Gospel but also of the natural law. For the natural law, too, declares the will of God, and its faithful observance is necessary for men's eternal salvation" (Pope Paul VI, On Human Life [*Humanae Vitae*], 4).

Christian Moral Living

Living Like Christ

Read aloud the following quote from St. John of the Cross. After a few moments of silent reflection, participants and sponsors may respond: "That which the soul aims at is equality in love with God, the object of its natural and supernatural desire. He who loves cannot be satisfied if he does not feel that he loves as much as he is loved" (*Spiritual Canticle of the Soul and the Bridegroom Christ*, Stanza 38).

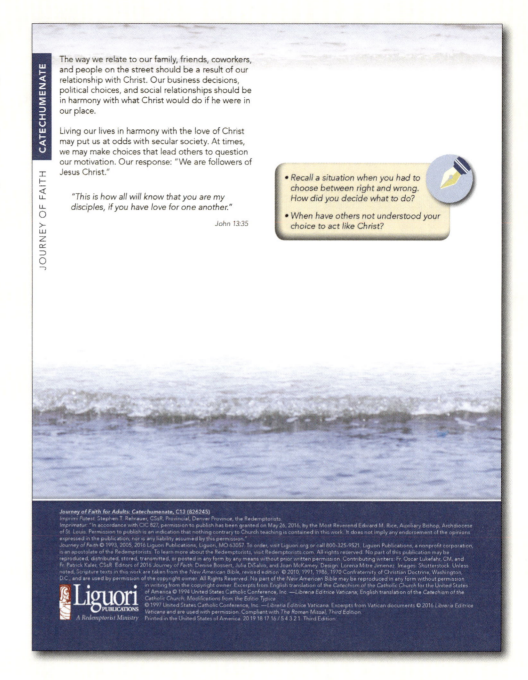

The way we relate to our family, friends, coworkers, and people on the street should be a result of our relationship with Christ. Our business decisions, political choices, and social relationships should be in harmony with what Christ would do if he were in our place.

Living our lives in harmony with the love of Christ may put us at odds with secular society. At times, we may make choices that lead others to question our motivation. Our response: "We are followers of Jesus Christ."

"This is how all will know that you are my disciples, if you have love for one another."

John 13:35

- Recall a situation when you had to choose between right and wrong. How did you decide what to do?
- When have others not understood your choice to act like Christ?

Journaling

Encourage participants to respond to the prompts and all the lesson's questions in their journals. Providing time for this work in the session will ensure that they are actively reflecting and forming their consciences while respecting their privacy.

Ask participants, "How has your conscience developed and matured since childhood and adolescence?" Explain that our concepts of morality and responsibility will naturally change as we enter adulthood. As participants better understand and consider the path of Christian moral living, remind them that the Christian definition of love—to love as Christ loves—is not how the world defines love. You may offer these additional prompts: *What does Christian love look like? How does a person with this kind of love act or respond?*

Closing Prayer

Dim the lights. Invite the participants make themselves comfortable. Keep the candle lit. Play the song "Restless" by Audrey Assad.

Looking Ahead

Summarize that the Church is our guide for applying Christ's teachings to changing and emerging issues in our own lives and around the world. Explain to participants that Christian morality is founded on the inherent dignity of all human life, which is discussed in lesson C14: *The Dignity of Life*. Have participants reflect on the many types and groups of people they encounter and how they tend to view and/or treat each one.

C13

Christian Moral Living

C14: The Dignity of Life

Catechism: 355–84, 1699–1729, 1877–1927, 2401–18

Objectives

Participants will…

- identify the inherent and universal nature of human dignity.

- recognize that all, especially Christians, are called to protect the rights and dignity of all people. This includes seeking to end economic injustice and societal structures that dehumanize, repress, or deny anyone's rights and dignity.

- recall several forms of prejudice—distinction based on race, creed, national origin, gender, sexual preference, age, ability, socioeconomic status, or political party and the Church's stance on the common good.

- recognize that the dignity of life also calls us to treat God's creation with respect and to answer the call to stewardship of that creation.

Leader Meditation

Luke 10:25–37

Thank God for the people in your life who have been Good Samaritans to you. Consider who might be the injured one you overlook because he or she is not part of your family, community, or culture. Think about simple, everyday ways that you can be a Good Samaritan to others.

Related *Catholic Updates*

- "The Gospel of Life: An Abbreviated Version of Pope John Paul II's Pro-life Encyclical" (C9509A)

- "What the Church Teaches About Homosexuality" (C9907A)

- "Pope Francis and the Environment" (C1509A)

Leader Preparation

- Read the lesson, this lesson plan, the opening Scripture, and the *Catechism* sections.

- Be familiar with the concepts of inherent or universal human dignity, prejudice, and human rights and freedoms as identified in the *Catechism* and within Catholic teaching. These terms and others like them are often understood and applied differently by participants and in political and secular contexts. You may have to clarify and return to foundational teachings throughout this session.

- Be familiar with historical and current events that center on issues of human dignity, life, and social justice. Use them as examples as you discuss the topics in this and the next two lessons, C14–C16. Avoid shifting the catechetical conversation to political debate.

Welcome

As you greet each person—whether catechumen, candidate, sponsor, spouse, or guest—take care to show equal courtesy and avoid favoritism. Explain that the next three lessons will discuss some sensitive and politically controversial subjects. Encourage them to remain open and honest and to listen actively both to others and to the teachings of the Church. Begin promptly.

Opening Scripture

Luke 10:25–37

Invite the participants to give examples of when someone took time from a busy life to help them in some way. Ask them, "How do acts of charity and kindness, no matter how small, reflect and contribute to human dignity?"

> The common good presupposes respect for the person as such. In the name of the common good, public authorities are bound to respect the fundamental and inalienable rights of the human person.
>
> *CCC 1907*

Journey of Faith for Adults, Catechumenate Leader Guide

In Short:

- The dignity of human life applies to all people.
- Protecting human dignity and rights is a duty of all Christians.
- Christians must condemn prejudice, promote the common good, and care for creation.

The Dignity of Life

Catholics believe that all people have been created by God, redeemed by Christ, and called to spend eternity with God. Most people agree that everyone must be treated equally, yet biases and discrimination on the basis of race, color, gender, age, ability, social condition, language, religion, and other factors remain common.

The spirituality of Christ demands that his followers take a stand against anything that dehumanizes, represses, or denies another person's rights and dignity. This means recognizing the dignity of all life and protecting human life from natural conception to natural death. It also means working to ensure that each person can live with dignity throughout life.

- When have you witnessed human dignity being affirmed? When have you witnessed human dignity being threatened or denied?
- What groups are the object of prejudice in your community?

Race and Ethnicity

We're living in a time when racial, ethnic, cultural, and linguistic diversity is more evident than ever. The face of the Church in this century will become even more ethnically diverse.

The U.S. bishops say that we—each of us—should live our opposition to racism daily and concretely. We should move others to oppose racism as well. In *Brothers and Sisters to Us*, the bishops condemn racism as "a radical evil that divides the human family and denies the new creation of a redeemed world." The bishops urge action by individuals, the Church, and society:

> "As individuals we should try to influence the attitudes of others by expressly rejecting racial stereotypes, racial slurs and racial jokes. We should influence the members of our families, especially our children, to be sensitive to the authentic human values and cultural contributions of each racial grouping in our country."
>
> *Brothers and Sisters to Us*

The Catholic Church in the U.S. is experiencing a profound demographic shift as communities of non-European origin are on the rise. Hispanics now make up about 35 percent of all Catholic adults in the U.S., and more than 25 percent of all U.S. Catholic parishes have Hispanic ministries. Studies suggest the Latino composition of our Church will continue to grow for decades to come. Consequently, monocultural parishes are being replaced by "shared parishes," that is, parishes in which more than one language, racial, or cultural group worship together as one Christian community.

CCC 355–84, 1699–1729, 1877–1927, 2401–18

The Dignity of Life

Invite participants to give real-life examples of people or groups who were wrongly treated and/or made to feel inferior because of how they were labeled.

Responses may include the treatment of blacks or American Indians throughout American history, the Holocaust of World War II, dowry deaths throughout the Indian subcontinent, and cases of tribal and religious genocide.

Clarify that while all humans have equal dignity and value, God does not desire or provide for uniformity. The natural law and diversity of spiritual gifts attest that not all are called to certain ministries or vocations. Furthermore, while our freedoms and rights can curb injustices, they will not (and should not) remove all worldly distinctions. Rather they exist to assist our *spiritual and moral pursuits*, which can be quite personal (CCC 1936–37).

Gender Equality

Reference the Letter of Pope John Paul II to Women (1995), a key document illustrating the Church's view of women, and review with participants if necessary.

Offer this *Catechism* quote to participants who seek the reason why women cannot be ordained: "Jesus chose men to form the college of the twelve apostles, and the apostles did the same when they chose collaborators to succeed them in their ministry.… The Church recognizes herself to be bound by this choice made by the Lord himself" (CCC 1577).

Sexual Orientation

Remind participants that human sexuality is rooted in the natural law and God's design of two complementary genders. For the sake of the spouses and family, intercourse and related sexual acts are reserved within a sacramental marriage. Reference lesson C8: *The Sacrament of Marriage*, if necessary, and note that lessons M2: *The Role of the Laity* and M7: *Family Life* will discuss marriage and the family further.

Read this authoritative statement if further clarification on the Church's relationship with those who identify as LGBT is needed: "Respect for homosexual persons cannot lead in any way to approval of homosexual behaviour or to legal recognition of homosexual unions. The common good requires that laws recognize, promote and protect marriage as the basis of the family, the primary unit of society. Legal recognition of homosexual unions…would mean not only the approval of deviant behaviour…but would also obscure basic values…" (Congregation for the Doctrine of the Faith, Considerations Regarding Proposals to Give Legal Recognition to Unions Between Homosexual Persons, 11).

Diversity is not something to overcome but is an essential component to foster. This can be an hour of great opportunity or a time of tragic disaster. As a people of God, we must learn to pray, work, and live together as an intercultural (not just multicultural) Church in which diversity provides an opportunity for growth and enrichment rather than separation and disunity. We need to affirm minority presence within the Church and acknowledge the gifts these cultures bring to the body of Christ.

"For you were slain and with your blood you purchased for God those from every tribe and tongue, people and nation."

Revelation 5:9

- How diverse is your parish?
- How well are minorities accepted and integrated into the life of the community?

Gender Equality

In the beginning, "God created mankind in his image; …male and female he created them" (Genesis 1:27). Human dignity applies equally to men and women. The *Catechism* says that when God created man and woman, he revealed two truths: the genders are distinct, and they have equal dignity (see CCC 369–70).

"Everyone, man and woman, should acknowledge and accept his [or her] sexual identity. Physical, moral, and spiritual difference and complementarity are oriented toward the goods of marriage and the flourishing of family life."

CCC 2333

- How can both men and women contribute their unique gifts to the faith life of the family?

Sexual Orientation

The Church provides pastoral guidance for those who identify as LGBT (lesbian, gay, bisexual, transgender) and those who care for them. Much of the teaching focuses on reaffirming the natural law and true nature of marriage and family and distinguishes between homosexual orientation and homosexual actions. The Church teaches that LGBT identification is objectively disordered and that the path of chastity—to which all of us are called according to our state in life—is the required route for avoiding sin.

"It is deplorable that homosexual persons have been and are the object of violent malice.… It reveals a kind of disregard for others which endangers the most fundamental principles of a healthy society. The intrinsic dignity of each person must always be respected in word, in action and in law."

Letter on the Pastoral Care of Homosexual Persons, 10 (published in 1986 at the direction of Pope John Paul II)

Socioeconomics

In its pastoral letter, Economic Justice for All: Catholic Social Teaching and the U.S. Economy, the U.S. bishops teach that economic decisions have moral and social dimensions, either enhancing or diminishing human dignity. Millions suffer the ravages of unmet needs, unrealized potential, and unfulfilled promises. The Church calls us to work toward building a just economy that works for all, and that includes food, security, work, affordable housing, and health care, tax assistance for low-income families, and programs for the poor and vulnerable.

The letter, published in 1986, proposes three questions that should form our economic perspectives:

- What does the economy do *for* people?
- What does it do *to* people?
- How do people *participate* in it?

Socioeconomics

Point out, if needed, that lesson C16: *Social Justice* will discuss this topic in greater detail, for instance, the rights of workers and our preference for the poor.

Journey of Faith for Adults, Catechumenate Leader Guide

"Part of the American dream has been to make this world a better place for people to live in; at this moment of history that dream must include everyone on this globe. Since we profess to be members of a 'catholic' or universal Church, we all must raise our sights to a concern for the wellbeing of everyone in the world."

Economic Justice for All, 363

As Christians, we must consider the consequences of our buying and saving habits not only on ourselves but on the whole world. Our financial systems and structures should promote the freedom and dignity of all persons and help them meet their basic needs.

- How might your economic choices have a negative impact on the poor? How might the gospel be calling you to make changes in your spending habits?

The Common Good

God created us to live in communion with the Trinity and each other. Within our communities, we mature, develop our abilities, and live out our Christian discipleship. In his encyclical On Christianity and Social Progress *(Mater et Magistra)*, Pope St. John XXIII explained that the common good includes "all those social conditions which favor the full development of human personality" *(MM* 65).

Such basic necessities as food, clothing, and shelter are included along with the rights to education, health care, taking an active part in public affairs, and worshiping God freely. Pope John stressed that the common good of one nation cannot be separated from the common good of the whole human family.

The *Catechism* lists three essential elements of the common good (CCC 1906–09):

1. *Respect for the person*. Societies should support individuals and communities in exercising their rights and freedoms and in fulfilling their vocations.

2. *Social well-being* and *development*. Authority should "arbitrate...between various particular interests; but it should make accessible to each what is needed."

3. *Peace* and *security*. Members should expect stability, and "authority should ensure...the right to legitimate personal and collective defense."

Care for Creation

"God looked at everything he had made, and found it very good."

Genesis 1:31

Christian concern extends beyond the human race to the fullness of God's creation. Protecting and caring for the environment begins with understanding the world as a shared gift from God. Social and economic development should benefit more and more people while sustaining all forms of life and respecting the laws of nature.

In his encyclical On Care for Our Common Home *(Laudato Si')*, Pope Francis says we're to be stewards of the earth for our benefit and that of future generations. He equates environmental abuse with sin, quoting Patriarch Bartholomew of Constantinople:

"For human beings to degrade the integrity of the earth by causing changes in its climate, by stripping the earth of its natural forests or destroying its wetlands; for human beings to contaminate the earth's waters, its land, its air, and its life—these are sins."

On Care For Our Common Home (Laudato Si'), 8

The Dignity of Life

Assist participants in researching upcoming events and/or share details on one you have selected or arranged (see "Looking Ahead," below). Point out that this activity may be delayed until after such time. Provide some time between this week and Pentecost to share and compare reactions and experiences.

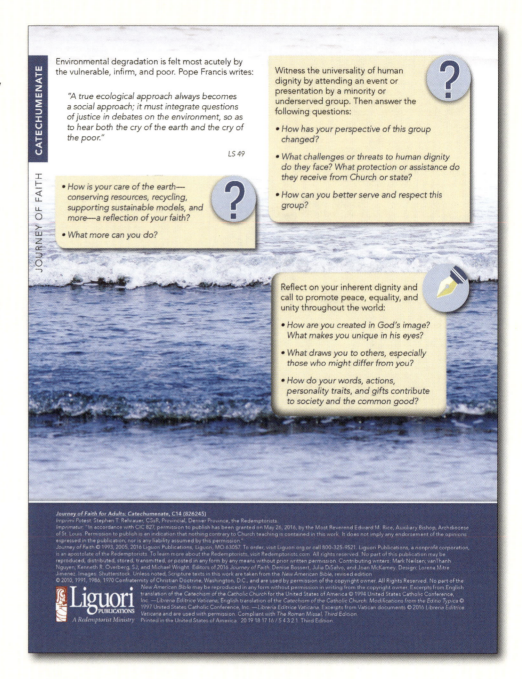

Journey of Faith for Adults, Catechumenate Leader Guide

Journaling

Have participants also reflect on their own prejudices, biases, assumptions, and insecurities. Most people have them, and awareness is a good first step toward changing our perspectives. Encourage them to answer these questions in their hearts, and praise their efforts:

• How can I weed out prejudice and labels from my own life? How can I sow seeds that bring about life and full appreciation for human dignity?

• Have I been the victim of prejudice or discrimination? What can I do to forgive others and to respond with gentle correction rather than judgment?

Closing Prayer

Invite participants to mention any special intentions, especially those that affect the dignity of the human person. Have a volunteer read Matthew 5:42–48; in this passage, Jesus asks that we treat everyone, even our enemies, with justice. Conclude by praying the Lord's Prayer together.

Looking Ahead

Explain that lesson C15: *A Consistent Ethic of Life* explores a wide variety of threats to the human person and emphasizes the need for a consistent pro-life position and social policy.

Invite the group to participate in an event or service project that exposes them to an overlooked part of society or promotes cultural awareness. Take advantage of parish and local activities, especially during Lent.

The Dignity of Life

C15: A Consistent Ethic of Life

Catechism: 1913–17, 2258–2330

Objectives

Participants will…

- recognize that all life is sacred
- identify issues that threaten a consistent ethic of life, including abortion, some reproductive technologies, euthanasia, war, capital punishment, torture, slavery, and human trafficking.
- describe an *intrinsically evil act* as one that is always morally wrong and never acceptable within human society.
- identify ways in which they can respect and defend life.

Leader Meditation

Genesis 1:24–31

Listen as the ancient authors speak of God as the author of all life. They proclaim that everything God made is sacred, beautiful, and good. Reflect on the power—and responsibility—inherent in this message. Ask yourself, "Is there some part of God's creation that I tend to overlook?" Spend a few minutes thanking God for the good things that you sometimes take for granted.

Related *Catholic Updates*

- "Abortion: What the Church Teaches" (C9808A)
- "End-of-Life Moral Issues" (C1407A)
- "What Is 'Just War' Today?" (C0405A)

Leader Preparation

- Read the lesson, this lesson plan, the opening Scripture, and the *Catechism* sections.
- Be familiar with the following vocabulary terms: consistent ethic of life, intrinsically evil act. Definitions are provided in this guide's glossary.
- Invite a member of your parish's pro-life committee or a local organization to attend the session and speak to participants about the challenges he or she faces in defending life and ways they can help and respect life in their own lives.

Welcome

Greet each person as he or she arrives. Check for supplies and immediate needs. Solicit questions or comments about the previous session and/or share new information and findings. Begin promptly.

Opening Scripture

Genesis 1:24–31

Light the candle and read the passage aloud. Discuss the intent of the inspired author. Ask, "What important truth was he trying to convey? What does this and other Scripture passages tell us about the value of all life, especially human life, in the eyes of God?"

Responses may include that all forms of life are good and valuable; that human life is unique, sacred, and placed above plant and animal life; that God called humans to care for all creatures and nature, especially each other. Also, Genesis 6—8 tells how God saved Noah and all creatures from the Flood, and Psalm 8 speaks of humanity's special standing.

> Human life is sacred because from its beginning it involves the creative action of God and it remains forever in a special relationship with the Creator, who is its sole end. God alone is the Lord of life from its beginning until its end.
> CCC 2258

Journey of Faith for Adults, Catechumenate Leader Guide

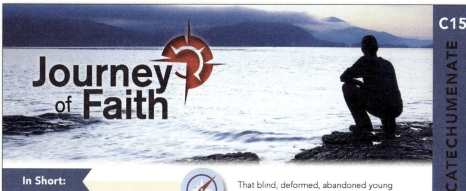

Journey of Faith

In Short:
- Many contemporary issues threaten human life.
- Some actions against life are intrinsically evil.
- Catholics are called to consistently defend all human life.

A Consistent Ethic of Life

In 1287, Margaret was born into an Italian noble family. She was blind and had a humpback, one leg shorter than the other, and an enlarged, misshapen head. Her parents told people she hadn't survived birth and banished her from the main rooms of their home. Margaret won the love of the servants with her intelligence and charm.

Fearing her identity might be revealed, her parents walled her into a tiny room in a chapel. Yet Margaret didn't lose heart. With the help of a priest, she learned to make her prison into a contemplative cell.

Margaret's parents took her to a city known for healing miracles. When no miracle occurred, they abandoned her at the church. Margaret didn't despair. Instead, she showed the love her parents denied her by giving love to the poor and needy. She became a Third Order Dominican, working to feed the hungry, care for the sick, and visit those in prison.

That blind, deformed, abandoned young woman made a difference in the world. Today, she is known as Blessed Margaret of Castello. Her life serves as a lesson about the sacredness and inherent value of *all* human life.

All Life Is Sacred

The Fifth Commandment clearly tells us, "You shall not kill" (Exodus 20:13; Deuteronomy 5:17). Following this commandment involves more than not committing murder. We must recognize and promote the dignity and sacredness of all human life.

Joseph Cardinal Bernardin called this all-embracing reverence for life a "**consistent ethic of life**," which includes opposition to abortion, massacre or genocide, capital punishment, and other sins against the dignity of the human person. It also includes support for social programs that feed the hungry, house the homeless, and help the elderly and immigrants.

> "A consistent ethic…argues for a continuum of life which must be sustained in the face of diverse and distinct threats. A consistent ethic does not say everyone in the Church must do all things, but it does say that as individuals and groups pursue one issue, whether it is opposing abortion or capital punishment, the way we oppose one threat should be related to support for a systemic vision of life."
>
> Joseph Cardinal Bernardin,
> 1984 address at Saint Louis University

CCC 1913–17, 2258–2330

A Consistent Ethic of Life

Invite the participants to share their reactions to the story of Blessed Margaret of Castello. Her practice (application) of a consistent ethic of life and heroic embrace of human dignity is an example to all. Ask, "What does this story teach us about our judgments on the value of human life? What are its implications with regard to abortion, euthanasia, embryonic stem-cell research, and capital punishment?" Remind them that in God's eyes, everyone is valuable.

Invite the group to share contemporary examples of pro-life choices—accepting an unplanned or crisis pregnancy, allowing death to take its natural course, forgiving an attacker—and individuals from their own lives or around the world who displayed such feats of heroic virtue and holiness. Acknowledge that these choices involve risk, real negative consequences, and a great deal of personal sacrifice, all of which witness to the truth and power of Christ's self-sacrifice on the cross.

All Life Is Sacred

Compare society's views on what makes human life valuable (beauty, intelligence, athletic ability, productivity) with the Church's view (that every human being is created by God in the image and likeness of God). Remind participants that a consistent ethic applies to *all* humans, even those who burden us and commit atrocious evils.

Ask, "Why is it so important that we regard every life as sacred? What problems are inherent in the idea of humans determining which lives are valuable and which are not?" Discuss the possible implications of having (or *not* having) a consistent ethic of life in today's world. Then ask, "Who has the authority to determine life or death? Where did this power come from?"

Responses may include that without a consistent ethic, forces of power and evil may overtake the weak and vulnerable, considering them unworthy and destroying them; individuals may be denied their right to fulfill their potential or receive healing and mercy; ultimately, only God determines life or death, though people—such as parents, health-care workers, and those in the military and law enforcement—can choose to cooperate with or act against God's will.

A Consistent Life Ethic

The Unborn

Point out, if needed, that unlike conception, neither implantation, birth, nor any other measure of viability can claim that it results in a new and distinct creature. This is a scientific (genetic) fact, not simply a religious or moral claim.

Explain that although abortion, in-vitro fertilization, embryonic stem-cell research, euthanasia, and capital punishment are sometimes proposed as common-sense or lesser-evil solutions to difficult problems, in reality they are rarely clear-cut and never fully altruistic (selfless) or universally beneficial.

Remind participants, if needed, that Catholic moral teaching asserts that conception must remain within the context of marriage and that all marriages must remain open to the possibility of new life. To that end, the Church opposes any practices that "dissociate the sexual act from the procreative act" (*CCC* 2377). This includes elective sterilization, surrogacy, contraceptives (especially abortifacient ones), fornication, and homosexual acts.

Reinforce the concept of an "intrinsically evil act" with examples from the lesson and Church documents. *Forming Consciences for Faithful Citizenship* by the United States Conference of Catholic Bishops (USCCB) identifies abortion, euthanasia, cloning, destructive embryonic research, and genocide—all of which are the intentional taking of life (22–23). A similar list and detailed explanation are found in Pope St. John Paul II's encyclical *Veritatis Splendor* (*VS* 79–83).

Clarify that Catholic teaching distinguishes between actions that are "intrinsically evil" (*always* morally wrong, regardless of intentions or outcome) and actions that, while morally problematic, may be justified in specific instances (for example, warfare and capital punishment). Emphasize that these labels are simply for the purpose of weighing competing goods and evils—such as in emergency or combat situations or when selecting a political candidate—and do not speak to any level of moral culpability. Such judgments are reserved for the proper authority (ultimately, a confessor and God) and must assess each individual case on its own.

Many of us affirm the sacredness of life in particular spheres that touch our hearts. Some are attracted to initiatives that protect the unborn. Others are drawn toward international peace organizations. No matter our cause or passion, we can each take concrete action in a way that supports all life.

> "We are facing an enormous and dramatic clash between good and evil, death and life, the 'culture of death' and the 'culture of life.' We find ourselves...with the inescapable responsibility of choosing to be unconditionally pro-life."
>
> Pope St. John Paul II, the Gospel of Life (Evangelium Vitae), 28

- What life issue do you feel strongly about?
- What challenges, if any, do you face in becoming "unconditionally pro-life?"

The Unborn

God gives each of us infinite value—distinct from our circumstances, productivity, or chance of worldly success. Created in God's image and likeness, each person can say to God: "You formed my inmost being; you knit me in my mother's womb" (Psalm 139:13). Jesus shows us that by receiving even little ones with love, we receive the Lord himself:

> "Taking a child [Jesus] placed it in their midst, and putting his arms around it he said to them, 'Whoever receives one child such as this in my name, receives me; and whoever receives me, receives not me but the One who sent me.'"
>
> Mark 9:36–37

Catholics must witness to the unique preciousness of each baby in the womb and provide families with practical assistance before and after birth. A mother's trust in God will grow as she experiences our support for life—both hers and her child's.

The Church has consistently taught that *abortion* is an **intrinsically evil act**, an action absolutely opposed to the will of God and the laws of nature and therefore never permissible.

The Church's position on life issues is founded in the understanding that human life begins at *conception* or *fertilization*—the fusion of sperm and ovum. In this moment, a unique being with its own soul and dignity is created. This has moral implications for a number of scientific and medical practices:

- embryonic stem-cell research
- human cloning
- some reproductive technologies, including *in vitro* fertilization and artificial insemination

In general, these acts involve the creation and subsequent destruction of human embryos. Regardless of their purpose, intention, or method, they equate to murder and are therefore unacceptable.

> "Because it should be treated as a person from conception, the embryo must be defended in its integrity, cared for, and healed like every other human being."
>
> CCC 2323

- How does your parish support efforts to end abortion and care for mothers in crisis pregnancies?

Journey of Faith for Adults, Catechumenate Leader Guide

The Suffering and Disabled

For the ancient Greek doctor Hippocrates, facilitating a person's death played no part in the practice of medicine: "I will not give a lethal drug to anyone if I am asked, nor will I advise such a plan" (Hippocratic Oath).

Current medical practices have introduced challenges to the question of life and death. Faced with greater possibilities for treatment and pain management, many become confused about what's appropriate. When youth, pleasure, and autonomy are presented as ideals, suffering is viewed as preventable and without meaning. Some assert a "right to die," to choose the time, place, and method of one's own death.

Catholic teaching is clear that **euthanasia**, the deliberate killing of the sick or impaired, is an intrinsically evil act. Withholding ordinary treatment such as nutrition and hydration from babies or adults with disabilities with intent to kill them is never allowed.

> "Nothing and no one can in any way permit the killing of an innocent human being, whether a fetus or an embryo, an infant or an adult, an old person, or one suffering from an incurable disease, or a person who is dying."
>
> Sacred Congregation for the Doctrine of the Faith, Declaration on Euthanasia, II

- How does allowing God to determine when life ends preserve the dignity of life?

The Innocent Victims of War

God created us to live in harmony. While Catholic teaching has always allowed for the legitimate defense of the innocent from unjust invasion, the nature of modern war has greatly increased the need to work for peace.

In the twentieth century, marked as it was by world wars and the use of atomic bombs, Catholic social teaching frequently turned to the topic of war and peace. Pope St. John XXIII's encyclical Peace on Earth (*Pacem in Terris*) emphasized human dignity, rights, and duties as the only possible foundation for peace. Vatican II's Pastoral Constitution on the Church in the Modern World (*Gaudium et Spes*) declared: "the arms race is an utterly treacherous trap for humanity, and one which ensnares the poor to an intolerable degree" (GS 81).

The twenty-first century has seen terrorist acts, civil wars, genocide, and wars between nations. In a January 2003 address to the diplomatic corps as the U.S. prepared for war against Iraq, Pope St. John Paul II stated: "War is not always inevitable. It is always a defeat for humanity." Pope Francis said:

> "War is never a satisfactory means of redressing injustice and achieving balanced solutions to political and social discord. All war is ultimately, as Pope Benedict XV stated in 1917, a 'senseless slaughter.' War drags peoples into a spiral of violence which then proves difficult to control; it tears down what generations have labored to build up and it sets the scene for even greater injustices and conflicts."
>
> Message at International Peace Meeting, August 26, 2014

The Innocent Victims of War

Refer to the *Catechism*'s "strict conditions for *legitimate defense by military force*" for a concise summary of the Church's just-war theory or doctrine (CCC 2309). Explain that given the dangers of modern weaponry and the many opportunities for diplomacy, deterrents such as international sanctions, and containment, war is very often avoidable and should be a last resort.

Mention that Pope St. John Paul II's 1991 encyclical *Centesimus Annus* (see especially 18) provides an excellent description of the real effects of modern war and argues for "genuine peace" and reconciliation rather than repudiation.

A Consistent Life Ethic

The Convicted Criminal

Emphasize that despite possible prejudices and errors in the course of due process, Christians are called to go beyond the letter of the law to a spirit of love that embraces God's divine mercy. Remind them that, like war, there are effective alternatives to ensuring the safety and rights of society short of killing.

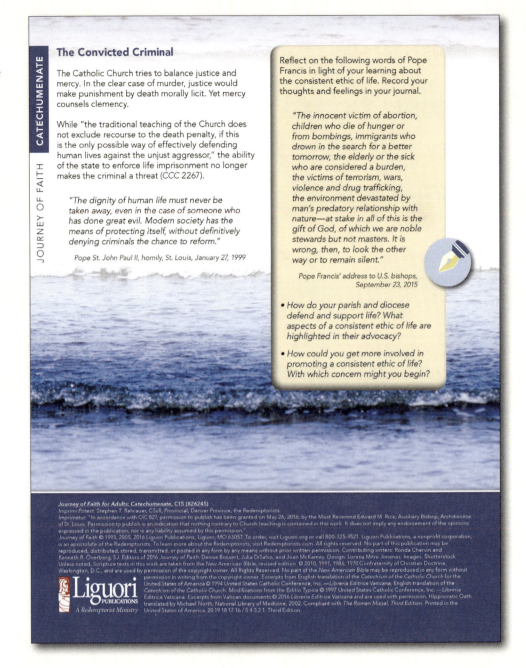

The Convicted Criminal

The Catholic Church tries to balance justice and mercy. In the clear case of murder, justice would make punishment by death morally licit. Yet mercy counsels clemency.

While "the traditional teaching of the Church does not exclude recourse to the death penalty, if this is the only possible way of effectively defending human lives against the unjust aggressor," the ability of the state to enforce life imprisonment no longer makes the criminal a threat (CCC 2267).

"The dignity of human life must never be taken away, even in the case of someone who has done great evil. Modern society has the means of protecting itself, without definitively denying criminals the chance to reform."

Pope St. John Paul II, homily, St. Louis, January 27, 1999

Reflect on the following words of Pope Francis in light of your learning about the consistent ethic of life. Record your thoughts and feelings in your journal.

"The innocent victim of abortion, children who die of hunger or from bombings, immigrants who drown in the search for a better tomorrow, the elderly or the sick who are considered a burden, the victims of terrorism, wars, violence and drug trafficking, the environment devastated by man's predatory relationship with nature—at stake in all of this is the gift of God, of which we are noble stewards but not masters. It is wrong, then, to look the other way or to remain silent."

Pope Francis' address to U.S. bishops, September 23, 2015

- How do your parish and diocese defend and support life? What aspects of a consistent ethic of life are highlighted in their advocacy?

- How could you get more involved in promoting a consistent ethic of life? With which concern might you begin?

Journey of Faith for Adults, Catechumenate Leader Guide

Journaling

Introduce and listen to the pro-life guest's presentation before the participants begin writing or responding to the prompts. This should inspire them and give them practical ideas from which to begin. Ask the participants and sponsors, "From what we just heard, where do you see Christ present and at work? What gives you hope?"

Closing Prayer

Bring to mind any special intentions—especially for the sick, dying, disabled, imprisoned, and unborn. (Specific intercessory prayers are available at the USCCB's website.) Thank God for the gift of life. Conclude with this excerpt from Birmingham (Alabama) Bishop Robert Baker's pro-life prayer:

Lord God,...You are the Protector and Defender of the lives of the innocent unborn...Change the hearts of those who compromise the call to protect and defend life. Bring our nation to the values that have made us a great nation, a society that upholds the values of life, liberty, and the pursuit of happiness for all. Amen.

Take-home

Encourage participants to support a pro-life group or resource in their region in a small way, even if just to pray for their ministry. This is especially meaningful during the month of January and/or Lenten season. If none are available nearby, consider ways to personally reach out to those in need. For those who prefer or are active in such causes already, lesson C16: "Social Justice" discusses ways to increase justice around the world and support other special groups, such as the poor and workers.

A Consistent Life Ethic

C16: Social Justice

Catechism: 1928–48, 2419–63

Objectives

Participants will…

- define social justice and recognize how it is founded on the teachings of Jesus Christ.
- identify the seven themes of Catholic social teaching.
- name practical ways that the laity can fulfill their call to advance social justice and advocate for the poor and vulnerable.
- learn that this area of Church teaching is constantly advancing to meet the needs of a changing society.

Leader Meditation

Luke 16:19–31

Think about times when you or a loved one felt like Lazarus. Who cared for you when you were most like Lazarus? How can you respond to the "Lazaruses" in your world? Keep in mind that your generous gifts of time, knowledge, and spiritual support in this RCIA ministry is indeed a response to the needs of others in and near God's Church.

Related *Catholic Updates*

- "100-plus Years of Catholic Social Teaching" (C9011A)
- "How Should We Think About the Poor" (C9207A)

Leader Preparation

- Read the lesson, this lesson plan, the Scripture passage, and the *Catechism* sections
- Be familiar with the following vocabulary terms: social justice, Catholic social teaching. Definitions are provided in this guide's glossary.
- If an election is approaching, gather copies of the USCCB's "Forming Consciences for Faithful Citizenship" or a related resource for each participant and sponsor.

Welcome

Greet the catechumens, candidates, and sponsors as they gather. Solicit questions or comments about the previous *two* sessions and/or share new information and findings. Begin promptly.

Opening Scripture

Luke 16:19–31

Light the candle and read the passage aloud. Discuss what the rich man could have done for Lazarus while they were both still alive. Ask the participants, "Why did the rich man ignore Lazarus?" Invite them to think about the people whom Lazarus represents in their own lives. Remind them of the different forms of poverty. People who lack friends, social standing, family stability, mental health, or love all experience a form of poverty.

> Society ensures social justice when it provides the conditions that allow associations or individuals to obtain what is their due, according to their nature and their vocation.
> *CCC 1928*

Journey of Faith for Adults, Catechumenate Leader Guide

Journey of Faith

C16 — CATECHUMENATE

In Short:

- The Church's social message is based on God's justice as expressed by Jesus.
- Catholic social teaching has seven key principles.
- Christians are called to promote justice and advocate for the poor and vulnerable.

Social Justice

From its beginning, the Catholic Church has sought to understand and live out Jesus' command to "love one another as I love you" (John 15:12). Following Christ's lead, the Church cares about the whole person. In addition to spiritual support and nourishment, the Church is called to provide food, shelter, and security to the needy. We're also called to work toward changing unjust systems so that the human rights of every person are met. This is our social responsibility.

> "The duty of making oneself a neighbor to others and actively serving them becomes even more urgent when it involves the disadvantaged, in whatever area this may be."
>
> *CCC 1932*

The Church's social message grows out of the conviction that each person has priceless value because we're created in God's image. No matter how poor, weak, sick, or powerless a person may be, he or she is to be treated as a child of God.

Christians are called to help establish **social justice** by ensuring that the basic needs required for a life of dignity are met for all people. These basic needs include food, clothing, shelter, and an income that supports the family. Christians are called to both share our gifts and cooperate with institutions that support the common good.

> "Make justice your aim: redress the wronged, hear the orphan's plea, defend the widow. Come now, let us set things right, says the Lord."
>
> *Isaiah 1:17–18*

> "You have been told, O mortal, what is good, and what the Lord requires of you: Only to do justice and to love goodness, and to walk humbly with your God."
>
> *Micah 6:8*

- What are some social justice issues you're aware of?
- Which ones do you feel strongly about? Why

Jesus and Social Justice

In the synagogue in Nazareth, Jesus read: "The Spirit of the Lord is upon me, because he has anointed me to bring glad tidings to the poor. He has sent me to proclaim liberty to captives and recovery of sight to the blind, to let the oppressed go free, and to proclaim a year acceptable to the Lord" (Luke 4:18–19; see Isaiah 61:1–2).

CCC 1928–48, 2419–63

ADULTS

Social Justice

Share examples, as a group, of injustice, oppression, and social inequality in our world today. They may exist in small or large areas, in our schools, workplaces, and in other countries. Emphasize that while we may feel powerless to fix the social injustices in our world, we have great power to effect social change within our families, churches, and neighborhoods.

Emphasize that living justly is a way of life, a habit we must begin early and practice daily. If time allows, read this statement from the *Catechism*: "*Justice* is the moral virtue that consists in the constant and firm will to give [our] due to God and neighbor….The just [person], often mentioned in the Sacred Scriptures, is distinguished by habitual right thinking and the uprightness of…conduct toward [one's] neighbor" (*CCC* 1807). Stress the word *habitual*. A truly just person is consistent in attitudes and behavior.

Discuss the statement: *Social responsibility begins with an attitude of respect for and generosity toward all peoples of the world.* Ask the participants, "How are human dignity and social justice interconnected?"

C16

Social Justice

The Church's Social Message

Mention that every presidential election year, the USCCB provides guidance on the political responsibility of Catholics through a document titled "Forming Consciences for Faithful Citizenship." Direct the group to this or a similar authoritative resource. If an election is approaching, distribute copies and take a few minutes to discuss its implications and possible applications.

Read the *Catechism*'s description of the purpose and meaning of work: "The primordial value of labor stems from man himself, its author and beneficiary. Work is for man, not man for work. Everyone should be able to draw from work the means of providing for his life and that of his family, and of serving the human community" (*CCC* 2428). Clarify that here, work can be defined broadly to include volunteer and domestic as well as professional pursuits (see Pope St. John Paul II's encyclical *Laborem Exercens*).

Emphasize that work and workers have value far beyond their productivity or revenue-generating capacity. Discuss how work can be a venue for experiencing human dignity. Encourage participants to reflect on how their work contributes to society and how it helps them develop as a person. Invite them to share times when their work has given purpose or structure to their lives. Ask, "How does unemployment or underemployment affect us emotionally as well as financially?"

Remind participants of the strides in worker's rights as mentioned in Pope St. John Paul II's encyclical *Centesimus Annus*: fair and living wages, safe and sanitary working conditions, "limitation of working hours," trade unions, and restrictions on child labor (*CA* 7–8).

Jesus took a stand for social justice. He was very aware of the pain and difficulties of real life. In Luke's Gospel (16:19–25), Jesus tells the story of Lazarus, a poor man who was "covered with sores," who longed to eat "the scraps that fell from the rich man's table."

When Lazarus died, he was "carried away by angels to the bosom of Abraham." When the rich man died and begged for mercy, Abraham responded, "My child, remember that you received what was good during your lifetime while Lazarus likewise received what was bad; but now he is comforted here, whereas you are tormented" (Luke 16:19–25).

In telling this story, Jesus isn't condemning the rich man because he was rich. The rich man's sin is that he closed his eyes to the suffering surrounding him. Jesus sends us a powerful message in this story: We are called to actively help the vulnerable, the poor, and the forgotten.

> "Why do you reject one who has the same rights over nature as you? It is not from your own goods that you give to the beggar; it is a portion of his own which you are restoring to him."
>
> St. Ambrose

- When have you been tempted to close your eyes to the suffering of another/others?
- How willing are you to take action and take a stand for the poor and oppressed? What are you willing to sacrifice: Your time? Your money? The esteem of others?

Prioritizing the Poor

Following Christ's example, the Church calls us to a *preferential love* for the poor (see *CCC* 2448). Our institutions, decisions, and actions should be guided by these four priorities, according to the U.S. bishops' pastoral letter Economic Justice for All (90–93):

1. Fulfillment of the basic needs of the poor.
2. Increase in the active participation of the poor and those on society's margins.
3. Greater investment of wealth and talent directed at benefiting the poor.
4. Evaluation of policies in light of their impact on family life.

> "Amen, I say to you, whatever you did for one of these least brothers of mine, you did for me....What you did not do for one of these least ones, you did not do for me."
>
> Matthew 25:40, 45

The Church's Social Message

Jesus wasn't a politician, but he didn't hesitate to speak out on political issues. The Church tries to follow his example. A true Christ-centered spirituality must condemn any structure, policy, or practice that diminishes or demeans people. The Church, therefore, must be who and what Jesus wants it to be: a leaven of peace, justice, and equality for all people, a defender of the dignity and rights of all God's people.

While asking the clergy and religious to refrain from holding political office, the Church doesn't avoid political issues, especially when human rights are threatened.

Journey of Faith for Adults, Catechumenate Leader Guide

The modern era of **Catholic social teaching** began with Pope Leo XIII's 1891 encyclical *On the Condition of Workers (Rerum Novarum)*. In response to changes in European society resulting from industrialization and urbanization, Pope Leo pleaded for an end to the exploitation of working people and called for a just and living wage and the right of workers to organize into unions and bargain collectively. Pope Leo also made it clear that Catholic tradition supports the right to private property and to a fair profit.

Since that time, the universal Church and national bishops conferences have spoken out about social issues such as war and peace, the economy, racism, religious freedom, capital punishment, the sanctity of life, hunger, poverty, and the environment. While Church leaders don't claim to be experts in economics, labor relations, or politics, they do understand the word of God regarding equality, justice, and human rights, and they call all people to understand and observe the law of God.

We're called to care both for the immediate needs of the poor through charitable works *and* to work to address the root causes of social problems through advocacy for just policies and helping change unjust social structures. Dorothy Day, cofounder of the Catholic Worker Movement, explained:

> "When you see a man walking on the road and he is run down by a truck, of course you will run to his aid. And if you see the same thing happen to another person, you will respond the same. And you would continue to respond to these scenes. But after a while, you would start to question where the trucks running people down are coming from. And when you found out, you would try to stop them at their source."
>
> Dorothy Day

- Why do you think many people are willing to "throw money" at social problems but unwilling to "get their hands dirty" through either direct service or advocacy?
- If all these things are needed, why isn't it enough for Christians to make charitable contributions?

Principles of Catholic Social Teaching

All Catholic social teaching grows out of the conviction that every person, as a beloved creation of God, has inherent value and dignity. The seven principles of Catholic social teaching guide our care for the needs and rights of all God's people.

Life and Dignity of the Human Person: All life must be protected from natural conception to natural death, and all forms of discrimination must end.

Call to Family, Community, and Participation: Traditional marriage and family life are the central social institutions and must be strengthened and supported.

Rights and Responsibilities: All people should have access to basic necessities of food, clothing, shelter, rest, medical care, and education.

Preferential Love for the Poor and Vulnerable: The needs of the poor and vulnerable come first and deserve our preferential response when we're in a position to help.

Principles of Catholic Social Teaching

Review the seven themes of Catholic social teaching. For each principle, solicit examples from participants of how we can affect social justice in the world.

Responses may include, but are not limited to, voting for socially responsible candidates and programs, donating our time and money to charitable organizations, supporting and assisting relatives and friends in need, and using our natural resources wisely and conservatively.

Social Justice

Dignity of Work and Rights of Workers: All people have a right to employment with adequate pay and decent working conditions.

Solidarity: We are one human family and must work for peace and justice for every person.

Care for God's Creation: We're called to protect human life and the world God has given to us.

- About which principle are you most concerned?
- What is God calling you to do about your concern?

The well-being of society is a concern of the Church and must be our concern as well.

We can participate in acts of social justice by:

1. *Sharing our goods.* Sharing what we have reduces the disparity between rich and poor.

2. *Serving others.* Jesus said whoever wishes to be great must become a servant (see Mark 10:42–45). We can volunteer to perform charitable works and acts of service.

3. *Standing up for justice.* We can select a social cause and take action to raise awareness of the need for change.

Read Matthew 25:31–46, then reflect on the following questions in your journal:

- How is God calling me to share my possessions with the needy?
- How is God calling me to serve others through charitable acts and acts of service?
- How is God calling me to stand up for justice?
- Who are the "least ones" crying for my attention today? How will I respond?

Journey of Faith for Adults: Catechumenate, C16 (826245)
Imprimi Potest: Stephen T. Rehrauer, CSsR, Provincial, Denver Province, the Redemptorists
Imprimatur: "In accordance with CIC 827, permission to publish has been granted on May 26, 2016, by the Most Reverend Edward M. Rice, Auxiliary Bishop, Archdiocese of St. Louis. Permission to publish is an indication that nothing contrary to Church teaching is contained in this work. It does not imply any endorsement of the opinions expressed in the publication, nor is any liability assumed by this permission."
Journey of Faith © 1993, 2005, 2016 Liguori Publications, Liguori, MO 63057. To order, visit Liguori.org or call 800-325-9521. Liguori Publications, a nonprofit corporation, is an apostolate of the Redemptorists. To learn more about the Redemptorists, visit Redemptorists.com. All rights reserved. No part of this publication may be reproduced, distributed, stored, transmitted, or posted in any form by any means without prior written permission. Contributing writers: Richard Schiblin, CSsR; Mark Neilsen; Joseph Morin, CSsR; Fr. Gary Ziuraitis, CSsR. Editors of 2016 Journey of Faith: Denise Bossert, Julia DiSalvo, and Joan McKamey. Design: Lorena Mitre Jimenez. Images: Shutterstock. Unless noted, Scripture texts in this work are taken from the *New American Bible,* revised edition © 2010, 1991, 1986, 1970 Confraternity of Christian Doctrine, Washington, D.C., and are used by permission of the copyright owner. All Rights Reserved. No part of the *New American Bible* may be reproduced in any form without permission in writing from the copyright owner. Excerpts from English translation of the *Catechism of the Catholic Church* for the United States of America © 1994 United States Catholic Conference, Inc. —Libreria Editrice Vaticana; English translation of the *Catechism of the Catholic Church: Modifications from the Editio Typica* © 1997 United States Catholic Conference, Inc. — Libreria Editrice Vaticana. Excerpts from Vatican documents © 2016 Libreria Editrice Vaticana and are used with permission. Compliant with *The Roman Missal, Third Edition.*
Printed in the United States of America. 20 19 18 17 16 / 5 4 3 2 1. Third Edition.

Liguori PUBLICATIONS
A Redemptorist Ministry

Journey of Faith for Adults, Catechumenate Leader Guide

Date	Handwritten note	Session	Event
Saturday, February 22, 2020			***Rite of Sending***
Sunday, February 23, 2020	11:30 am St. Joes		
Wednesday, February 26, 2020			**ASH WEDNESDAY (Attending Mass Together)**
Saturday, February 29, 2020	2 pm		***Rite of Election (At Blessed Sacrament Cathedral, Detroit)***
Sunday, March 01, 202			
Wednesday, March 04, 2020		L2-	Living Lent
Saturday, March 07, 2020	…thew gone		***Penitential Rite of Candidates***
Sunday, March 08, 2020	930 St. Pats		
Wednesday, March 11, 2020	? Reconciliat… w/ father Brend…	L3-	Scrutinies: Looking Within
Saturday, March 14, 2020	4pm St. Joes		**First Scrutiny for Elect**
Sunday, March 15, 2020			
Wednesday, March 18, 2020		L4-	The Creed
Satruday, March 21, 2020			***Second Scrutiny for Elect***
Sunday, March 22, 2020	1130 St. Joes		
Wednesday, March 25, 2020		L5-	The Way of the Cross
Satruday, March 28, 2020			***Third Scrutiny for Elect***
Sunday, March 29, 2020	930 am St. pats		
Wednesday, April 01, 2020		L6-	The Lord's Prayer
Saturday, April 04, 2020	930-1230 Riverhouse		***RCIA RETREAT***
Sunday, April 05, 2020			***PALM SUNDAY***
Wednesday, April 08, 2020		L7-	The meaning of Holy Week
Thursday, April 09, 2020			HOLY THURSDAY
Friday, April 10, 2020			GOOD FRIDAY
Satruday, April 11, 2020	8pm St. Joes		***Easter Vigil (POT LUCK after)***
Sunday, April 12, 2020			Easter Sunday
Wednesday, April 15, 2020		**OFF**	**REFLECTING OF WHAT YOU JUST WENT THROUGH**
Wednesday, April 22, 2020	…dd caden + zoey	E1-	Conversion: A lifelong Process
Wednesday, April 29, 2020		E2-	The Role of the Laity
Wednesday, May 06, 2020		E3-	Your Spiritual Gifts
		E4-	Discernment
Wednesday, May 13, 2020		E5-	Our Call to Holiness
		E6-	Living the Virtues
Wednesday, May 20, 2020		E7-	Family Life
		E8-	Evangelization
Wednesday, May 27, 2020			***RCIA Family Dinner***

Laura Lowrey

~ Catechist In-Service ~

Catechist Charism Workshop

Tuesday, January 7, 2020

St Joseph Hall

6:00pm-6:30pm Dinner

6:30pm-8:30pm Presenter, Mary Garlow

Mary Garlow, from Via Maria Consulting, LLC has years of experience in Pastoral Ministry. She's held positions as Senior Consultant with the Spritzer Center for Ethical Leadership, Coordinator of Evangelization for the Archdiocese of Detroit, Youth Minister Coordinator at the National Shrine of the Little Flower, Director of Religious Education at Our Lady of Sorrows and Our Lady Queen of Martyrs Church in Beverly Hills where she is currently employed.

Mary is trained in the *Called & Gifted* spiritual gifts discernment process, is a certified teacher and interviewer as well. At this workshop she will help all that attend to recognize their spiritual gifts and strengths. The evening promises to be enlightening and most important a spiritually uplifting evening. Please make every effort to attend.

The parish has covered the cost of dinner and Via Maria Consulting's compensation fee of $300. There is an individual cost of $5 per person we are asking each of you to cover for the materials she will provide ahead of time to evaluate your personal gifts.

Please return this form with your $5 no later than Tuesday, December 10th. Mary needs sufficient time to issue each of you a self-evaluation form and to get it back to her.

✂ ~~~~~~

Please return this portion no later than Dec. 10

Catechist Charism Workshop ~ January 7, 2020

NAME: _____

PHONE: _____

YES, I WILL ATTEND: DINNER-6pm_____   WORKSHOP-6:30pm_____

$5 IS ENCLOSED_____   WILL PAY LATER_____

I REGRET I CANNOT ATTEND: _____

2017 - 2018 RCIA Schedule
St. Vincent Pallotti Parish

Date	Lesson / Event
Saturday, October 07, 2017	**Rite of Welcoming and Acceptance**
Sunday, October 08, 2017	
Monday, October 09, 2017	C1 - The RCIA Process and Rites
Monday, October 16, 2017	C2 - The Sacraments
Monday, October 23, 2017	C3 - The Sacrament of Baptism
Monday, October 30, 2017	C4 - The Sacrament of Confirmation
Monday, November 06, 2017	C5 - The Sacrament of Eucharist
Monday, November 13, 2017	C6 - The Sacrament of Penance and Reconciliation
Monday, November 20, 2017	C7 - The Sacrament of the Anointing of the Sick
	C8 - The Sacrament of Marriage
Sunday, November 26, 2017	Christ the King
Monday, November 27, 2017	C8 - The Sacrament of Marriage
Monday, December 04, 2017	C9 - The Sacrament of Holy Orders
Monday, December 11, 2017	C10 - The People of God
Monday, December 18, 2017	**Off - Christmas / New Year Break**
Monday, December 25, 2017	**Off - Christmas / New Year Break**
Monday, January 01, 2018	**Off - Christmas / New Year Break**
Monday, January 08, 2018	C11 - The Early Church
Monday, January 15, 2018	C12 - History of the Church
Monday, January 22, 2018	C13 - Christian Moral Living
Monday, January 29, 2018	C14 - The Dignity of Life
	C15 - The Consistent Life Ethic
Monday, February 05, 2018	C16 - Social Justice
Sunday, February 11, 2018	**Rite of Sending**
Monday, February 12, 2018	L1 - What Is Lent?
Wednesday, February 14, 2018	**Ash Wednesday**
Saturday, February 17, 2018	**Rite of Election (At Blessed Sacrament Cathedral, Detroit)**
Sunday, February 18, 2018	

Journaling

Emphasize that we cannot remain silent in the face of injustice. Have participants reflect in their prayer journals on ways they can live out the gospel and permit those things that Jesus cares about to become the very things they care about as well. Have them choose one person this week who will be Jesus to them. Encourage them to write about their experience of caring for the "Christ" they encounter this week.

Closing Prayer

After the participants voice any special intentions, proclaim Matthew 25:31–40, in which Jesus tells us that when we show care and concern for the least of our brothers and sisters, we show love and concern for him.

Looking Ahead

Have participants review the seven themes of Catholic social teaching and select one on which to focus their prayer and almsgiving during Lent.

Remind participants and sponsors, if applicable, that this lesson concludes the Catechumenate series. Remind them that as participants draw closer to the Easter Vigil, their spiritual journey will intensify. Be sure to present lesson E1: *Election: Saying Yes to Jesus* prior to the rite of election.

C16

Social Justice

Journey of Faith for Adults
Catechumenate Glossary (alphabetical)

absolution (C6): In the sacrament of penance, the form or words spoken by the priest that "grants the penitent 'pardon and peace,'" "remits the guilt and penalty due to sin," and restores his or her state of grace (*CCC* 1424; *Modern Catholic Dictionary*). "Through the prayer and ministry of the Church," God, "the Father of mercies," pardons the sinner who, in confession, has shared remorse for his or her sins, the desire to do better and/or to make amends, and performs the penance (*CCC* 1449).

act of contrition (C6): In the sacrament of penance, a prayer, often formulaic, that expresses sorrow for sin. It is recited between the acceptance of the penance and the conferral of absolution. "Repentance (also called contrition) must be inspired by motives that arise from faith. If repentance arises from love of charity for God, it is called 'perfect' contrition; if it is founded on other motives, it is called 'imperfect'" (*CCC* 1492).

anointing of the sick (C7): The ritual act of smearing, rubbing, or pouring blessed oil upon a person, such as someone who's sick, or an object. Traditionally, anointing has been used for sanctification (for example, priests, prophets, kings, altars, sacred vessels; see Exodus 28:41, 29:36, 30:25–32; and 1 Samuel 10:1 and 16:13). Anointing the sick not only comforts the afflicted and soothes the injury in the hope of healing or cure but also strengthens the person's faith to endure suffering or death and unites it with Christ's redemptive passion and death. As a sacrament of healing, the Church offers it to any of the faithful who are "in danger due to sickness or old age" (Canon 1004). The

essential rite consists of a priest's laying hands upon the person, anointing the forehead with oil, and prayers. It can be received more than once depending on the person's changing condition.

baptism (C3): From the Greek for "immersion"; the primary Christian sacrament, through which individuals are "freed from sin and reborn as sons of God; we become members of Christ, are incorporated into the Church and made sharers in her mission" (*CCC* 1213). The essential rite consists of the pouring of, or immersion into, water and the Trinitarian formula "I baptize you in the name of the Father, and of the Son, and of the Holy Spirit" (*RCIA* 317; *Rite of Baptism for Children*, 60). Other elements include anointing with oil, a profession of faith, clothing with a white garment, and lighting a candle from the Easter candle. Godparents "present the child to the Church" with the parents and represent the faith community (*Rite of Baptism for Children*, 33).

candidate (C1): Within the RCIA a baptized Christian who desires and is preparing to come into full communion with the Catholic Church. Candidates may be received into the Church at the Easter Vigil or on another Sunday during the year depending on his or her circumstances and readiness. The process and rites for candidates are distinct from that of unbaptized catechumens. Also, a baptized Catholic, often an adolescent, who is preparing for the sacrament of confirmation.

Catholic social teaching (C16): The unified and ongoing social tradition and doctrine of the Church, "which is articulated as the Church interprets events in the course of history…in the light of the whole of what has been

revealed….The Church's social teaching proposes principles for reflection; it provides criteria for judgment; it gives guidelines for action" (*CCC* 2422–23). It can be summarized and understood according to its seven key themes.

chalice (C9): An ornate, cuplike sacred vessel that holds the wine to be consecrated into the Precious Blood at Mass. The celebrant elevates the chalice, though additional, often less ornate, communion cups may also be used for distribution.

chastity (C8): "The successful integration of sexuality within the person….The chaste person maintains the integrity of the powers of life and love placed in him" (*CCC* 2337–38). This moral virtue and fruit of the Spirit "comes under the cardinal virtue of *temperance*" and calls all to self-mastery, purity, and modesty (*CCC* 2341, 2345). "'People should cultivate [chastity] in the way that is suited to their state of life. Some profess virginity or consecrated celibacy….' Married people are called to live conjugal chastity; others practice chastity in continence" (*CCC* 2349). Conjugal chastity calls spouses to fidelity and to honoring the unitive and procreative natures of each act.

chrism (C3): Olive oil mixed with balsam that has been blessed (consecrated) by the bishop at the chrism Mass for use in the sacraments of baptism, confirmation, and during the ordination of a priest or bishop. This sacramental is also called *sacred chrism*.

common priesthood (C9): A spiritual grace and consecration received by all Christians at baptism. "The common priesthood of the faithful is exercised by the unfolding of baptismal

104

grace…, the ministerial [ordained] priesthood is at the service of the common priesthood" (*CCC* 1547. This priesthood calls for "full, conscious, and active participation in liturgical celebrations," including those *particular ministries* available to the laity, such as "servers, lectors commentators, and members of the choir" (*CCC* 1141, 1143; see *Sacrosanctum concilium*, 29; and Dogmatic Constitution on the Church [*Lumen Gentium*], 10).

confirmation (C4): From the Latin for "strengthen"; the sacrament of initiation that deepens and completes baptismal grace and strengthens the individual with the Holy Spirit for mature discipleship. The essential rite consists of an anointing with oil and laying on of hands by the bishop or priest and the words, "Be sealed with the Gift of the Holy Spirit" (*The Order of Confirmation*). Those who are baptized as adults and older children receive confirmation along with baptism; those baptized as infants receive confirmation at the "age of discretion," which often . corresponds with adolescence (Canon 891).

conscience (C13): "Moral conscience, present at the heart of the person, enjoins him at the appropriate moment to do good and to avoid evil. It also judges particular choices, approving those that are good and denouncing those that are evil….Conscience is a judgment of reason whereby the human person recognizes the moral quality of a concrete act that he is going to perform, is in the process of performing, or has already completed….It is by the judgment of his conscience that man perceives and recognizes the prescriptions of the divine law" (*CCC* 1777–78).

consistent ethic of life (C15): As first articulated by Joseph Cardinal Bernardin in a lecture at Fordham University in 1983, the belief that all human life is sacred, that all

humans have dignity, and that our actions should reflect this. It is commonly associated with life issues, including those that involve "direct and intentional killing," such as intentional homicide, abortion, euthanasia, unjust war, and capital punishment (*CCC* 2268; see **intrinsically evil act**).

crosier (C9): "An ornamental staff shaped like a shepherd's crook. It may be held or carried by bishops, mitered abbots, and other privileged prelates. It symbolizes a bishop's role as caretaker of his flock" (*Modern Catholic Dictionary*).

denomination (C12): A group or branch of Christianity (or any religion) with its own rules of governance and bodies of authority. Many Christian denominations are associated with the Protestant Reformation and have therefore split from and lost full communion with the Catholic Church.

elect (C1): The name given to catechumens who have gone through the rite of election, have entered the period of purification and enlightenment, and are preparing to celebrate the sacraments of initiation (baptism, confirmation, and the Eucharist) at the next Easter Vigil.

examination of conscience (C6): A prayerful reflection over one's words and deeds using the Gospel and commandments as a guide, to determine where one has sinned against God. While regular, even daily, examinations (such as St. Ignatius' general *Examen*) can be spiritually beneficial, an examination of conscience should be done prior to the sacrament of penance (*CCC* 1454).

exodus (C10): The departure of the Israelites from Egypt as recounted in the Book of Exodus. Moses guided the Hebrews out of slavery and through the wilderness to Mount Sinai, where God handed down the Ten Commandments.

Moses died before they reached their ultimate destination: the Promised Land.

grace (C2): "*Favor*, the *free and undeserved help* that God gives us to respond to his call to become children of God…. Grace is a *participation in the life of God*….This vocation to eternal life is *supernatural*," a "gratuitous gift" (*CCC* 1996–99). The Church distinguishes several types of grace, such as *sanctifying grace*, sometimes called *justifying* or *habitual grace*; *actual graces*; *sacramental graces*; and *special graces* (*CCC* 1996–2005; see also C2 lesson plan).

heresy (C12): "The obstinate post-baptismal denial of some truth which must be believed with divine and catholic faith" (*CCC* 2089; see also Canon 751). Also, false teachings and proclamations that directly contradict Church doctrine and divine revelation. Cases of formal heresy, in which a baptized person knowingly rejects such a truth (yet still professes a Christian faith, otherwise it constitutes *apostasy*), are considered a grave sin and may result in excommunication. In cases of material heresy, when a baptized person accepts heretical doctrine in good faith and does not knowingly reject the truth, there is no sin.

intrinsically evil act (C15): an act that is always opposed to the authentic good of God's creation and therefore always morally wrong. These acts must always be opposed and avoided. An example of an intrinsically evil act is abortion, which is the intentional taking of an innocent life (see *CCC* 2271–72).

missionary (C11): From the Latin for "sent"; one who goes out to spread the good news of Jesus' death and resurrection, and of his presence in the Church to those who would not otherwise hear it. Traditionally missionaries traveled to foreign countries, but anyone who actively evangelizes the good news of Jesus and his Church can be considered a missionary. In fact, the Church's very nature is missionary.

miter (C9): An ornate liturgical headdress worn by a bishop or abbot. It is tall, pointed at the top, and has two hanging flaps in the back.

mortal sin (C6): A grave (serious) sin which "destroys charity in the heart [and] turns man away from God....[It] necessitates a new initiative of God's mercy and a conversion of heart which is normally accomplished within [the] sacrament of reconciliation.... For a *sin* to be *mortal*, three conditions must together be met: 'Mortal sin is sin whose object is grave matter and which is also committed with full knowledge and deliberate consent" (*CCC* 1855–57). If one is guilty of mortal sin (has not confessed and received absolution), Eucharist cannot be received. For this and other reasons, the Church calls its members to confess all mortal sins in kind and number in the sacrament of penance.

natural family planning (C8): "The controlling of human conception by restricting the marital act to the infertile periods of the wife" (*Modern Catholic Dictionary*). In practice, NFP involves the observation and tracking of various biological signs in the woman to determine the period of ovulation. Today, many scientific, effective, and morally permissible methods are available. Most assist couples in monitoring cervical mucus, basal body temperature, hormone levels, or a combination thereof. NFP methods can also be used to achieve pregnancy and to monitor or diagnose the woman's reproductive health.

neophyte (C1): In the context of the RCIA, one who has been "newly planted" in the faith through the sacrament of baptism; a newly baptized Catholic Christian.

ordination (C9): "The sacrament through which the mission entrusted by Christ to his apostles continues to be exercised in the Church until the end of time: thus it is the sacrament of apostolic ministry. It includes three degrees: episcopate [bishops], presbyterate [priests], and diaconate [deacons]" (*CCC* 1536). Ordination "confers a gift of the Holy Spirit that permits the exercise of a 'sacred power' (*sacra potestas*) which can come only from Christ himself through his Church....The *laying on of hands* by the bishop, with the consecratory prayer, constitutes the visible sign of this ordination" (*CCC* 1538). Also known as *holy orders*.

original sin (C3): The state "deprived of original holiness and justice" in which all people are conceived and inherit from Adam and Eve (*CCC* 404–05, 416–17). "Although he was made by God in a state of holiness,... man finds that he has inclinations toward evil [concupiscence] too, and is engulfed by manifold ills which cannot come from his good Creator" (Pastoral Constitution on the Church in the Modern World [*Gaudium et Spes*], 13; see also *CCC* 1264, 1426). Original sin is removed in the sacrament of baptism.

Passover (C10): The Lord's tenth and final plague against Egypt, in which every firstborn Egyptian child and animal died but the Israelites were passed over, ensuring their safety and imminent freedom from slavery (Exodus 11–12). Also, the ritual meal established by God for this event and the Jewish feast commemorating it. "Jesus chose the time of Passover to fulfill what

he had announced at Capernaum: giving his disciples his Body and his Blood....By celebrating the Last Supper with his apostles in the course of the Passover meal, Jesus gave the Jewish Passover its definitive meaning" (*CCC* 1339–40). In the Eucharist, Christ is our paschal (Passover) lamb, our eternal Savior, and our food for the journey, our "bread of life" (John 6:32–51).

paten (C9): A flat, platelike sacred vessel, usually covered in gold or silver, on which hosts to be consecrated in the Mass are placed.

penance (C6): "Visible signs, gestures and works" that reflect a person's remorse for his or her sins, interior conversion, and attempt to make amends (*CCC* 1430). The most common Christian penances are fasting, prayer, and almsgiving, particularly during Lent (*CCC* 1434). One also may perform penances for others, including the faithful departed in purgatory (*CCC* 1032). In the early Church, public penance was expected prior to reconciliation (*CCC* 1447). Today the term *penance* is associated with the sacrament, specifically the required instruction given by the priest before the act of contrition. This penance, along with "confession to a priest" and his prayer of absolution, is "an essential part of the sacrament" (*CCC* 1456).

Pentecost (C11): The descent of the Holy Spirit on the apostles and the baptism of an estimated 3,000 new Christians (Acts 2:1–41). On that day, the Spirit was "manifested, given, and communicated as a divine person....On that day, the Holy Trinity is fully revealed" (*CCC* 731–32; see also lesson Q3). Also, the liturgical solemnity, held fifty days after Easter and officially ending the Easter season, which commemorates this event. It recognizes and celebrates God's establishment (birth) of the Christian Church and its missionary nature.

presentation of the Creed (C1): A celebration that marks the elect's acceptance and belief of everything the Creed states and in which the Church "lovingly entrusts to them…the ancient texts that have always been regarded as expressing the heart of the Church's faith and prayer" (*RCIA* 147). It generally takes place in the week following the first scrutiny (during the period of purification and enlightenment). During the Easter Vigil or a preparation rite on Holy Saturday, the elect will recite and profess either the Nicene or Apostles' Creed.

presentation of the Lord's Prayer (C1): Another presentation to the elect that "fills them with a deeper realization of the new spirit of adoption by which they will call God their Father, especially in the midst of the eucharistic assembly" (*RCIA* 147). It is generally celebrated "during the week after the third scrutiny" (*RCIA* 21, 178).

rite of acceptance (C1): "The liturgical rite…marking the beginning of the catechumenate proper, as the candidates express and the Church accepts their intention to respond to God's call to follow the way of Christ" (*Christian Initiation of Adults*, Part I). Through this rite, unbaptized inquirers become catechumens and "are now part of the household of Christ" (*RCIA* 47). Prior to the rite, each inquirer must select a sponsor and show "evidence of the first faith…of the first stirrings of repentance, a start to the practice of calling upon God in prayer, a sense of the Church, and some experience of the company and spirit of Christians through contact with a priest or with members of the community" (*RCIA* 42; see *Journey of Faith for Adults Inquiry Leader Guide*).

rite of election (C1): "The liturgical rite, usually celebrated on the first Sunday of Lent, by which the Church formally ratifies the catechumens' readiness for the sacraments of initiation and the catechumens, now the elect, express the will to receive these sacraments" (*RCIA* Part I). Through this rite, the elect enter the period of purification and enlightenment. Prior to this rite, each catechumen must have selected a godparent, "have undergone a conversion in mind and in action and [have] developed a sufficient acquaintance with Christian teaching as well as a spirit of faith and charity" (*RCIA* 120). Also called *the enrollment of names* (see "Belonging to the Catechumenate" in this guide and *Journey of Faith for Adults Inquiry Leader Guide*).

rite of welcoming (C1): The liturgical rite which "welcomes baptized but previously uncatechized adults who are seeking to complete their Christian initiation through the sacraments of confirmation and Eucharist or to be received into the full communion of the Catholic Church" (*RCIA* 411). After receiving this rite, candidates regularly attend Sunday Eucharist and/or celebrations of the word of God and prepare for further rites and celebrations leading to full reception. Liturgically, this rite is similar to the rite of acceptance (see *RCIA* 411–33).

sacrament (C2): "An outward sign instituted by Christ to give grace" (*Baltimore Catechism*). Through each sacrament, the Holy Spirit manifests (effects) its particular grace for the good of the recipient and the whole Church. The Catholic Church celebrates seven sacraments: baptism, confirmation, Eucharist, penance and reconciliation, anointing of the sick, matrimony (marriage), and holy orders. Each sacrament has a proper *matter* (material and/or action), *form* (conferring ritual and/

or words), and *minister* in order to be valid.

schism (C12): From the Greek for "split"; the division of two parties or formal separation (secession) of a faction due to differences in belief. In particular, "the refusal of submission to the Supreme Pontiff or of communion with the members of the [Catholic] Church subject to him" (Canon 751; see also *CCC* 2089, 817). The *Great Schism* refers to the Eastern (Orthodox) Church's breaking from the Western (Roman/Latin) Church beginning in 1054.

scrutinies (C1): Three rites for the unbaptized elect that usually occur on the Third, Fourth, and Fifth Sundays of Lent. "The scrutinies are meant to uncover, then heal all that is weak, defective, or sinful in the hearts of the elect; to bring out, then strengthen all that is upright, strong, and good….[The elect] are expected particularly to progress in genuine self-knowledge through serious examination of their lives and true repentance" (*RCIA* 141–42). The rites feature and reflect on the Gospel readings from Sunday Cycle A "and are reinforced by an exorcism" (*RCIA* 141; see *Journey of Faith for Adults Inquiry Leader Guide*).

sin (C6): "Failure in genuine love for God and neighbor caused by a perverse attachment to certain goods….Sin is an offense against God….Like the first sin, it is disobedience, a revolt against God…" (*CCC* 1849–50). Sin is "an abuse of the freedom that God gives to created persons" (*CCC* 387; see **mortal sin** and **venial sin**).

social justice (C16): An act or state in which individuals and institutions serve the common good, respect the rights and dignity of all, and "obtain what is their due, according to their nature and their vocation" (*CCC* 1928).

transubstantiation (C5):
The conversion "of the whole substance of the bread into the substance of the body of Christ our Lord, and of the whole substance of the wine into the substance of His blood" (Council of Trent, Session 13, chapter 4; see *CCC* 1376). The Catholic Church uses this term to describe its belief that "after the consecration of the bread and wine, our Lord Jesus Christ, true God and man, is truly, really, and substantially contained under the species of those sensible things" (Council of Trent, Session 13, chapter 1; see *CCC* 1374). Though the appearances (taste, smell, physical appearance) of bread and wine remain, both species of the Eucharist truly and fully contain the *Body, Blood, soul, and divinity* of Christ.

venial sin (C6): An offense against God that "does not deprive the sinner of sanctifying grace, friendship with God, charity and therefore eternal happiness" (Pope St. John Paul II, Reconciliation and Penance, 17; see *CCC* 1863). "One commits venial sin when, in a less serious matter, he does not observe the standard prescribed by the moral law, or when he disobeys the moral law in a grave matter, but without full knowledge or without complete consent" (*CCC* 1862). "Regular confession of our venial sins helps us form our conscience, fight against evil tendencies, let ourselves be healed by Christ and progress in the life of the Spirit" (*CCC* 1458).